P9-BZR-316

START & RUN A REAL
HOME-BASED BUSINESS

START & RUN A REAL HOME-BASED BUSINESS

Dan Furman

Self-Counsel Press
(a division of)
International Self-Counsel Press Ltd.
USA   Canada

Copyright © 2007 by International Self-Counsel Press Ltd.

All rights reserved.

No part of this book may be reproduced or transmitted in any form by any means — graphic, electronic, or mechanical — without permission in writing from the publisher, except by a reviewer who may quote brief passages in a review.

Self-Counsel Press acknowledges the financial support of the Government of Canada through the Book Publishing Industry Development Program (BPIDP) for our publishing activities.

Printed in Canada.

First edition: 2007

Library and Archives Canada Cataloguing in Publication

Furman, Dan, 1966–
    Start & run a real home-based business / Dan Furman.

(Self-counsel business series)
Includes a CD-ROM.
ISBN 978-1-55180-784-3

    1. New business enterprises. 2. Home-based businesses. I. Title.
II. Title: Start and run a real home-based business. II. Series.

HD62.5.F868 2007   658.1'1   C2007-902686-9

ANCIENT FOREST FRIENDLY Self-Counsel Press is committed to protecting the environment and to the responsible use of natural resources. We are acting on this commitment by working with suppliers and printers to phase out our use of paper produced from ancient forests. This book is one step toward that goal. It is printed on 100 percent ancient-forest-free paper (30 percent post-consumer recycled), processed chlorine- and acid-free.

Self-Counsel Press
(a division of)
International Self-Counsel Press Ltd.

1704 North State Street
Bellingham, WA 98225
USA

1481 Charlotte Road
North Vancouver, BC V7J 1H1
Canada

Contents

Notice to Readers

The author, the publisher, and the vendor of this book make no representations or warranties regarding the outcome or the use to which the information in this book is put and are not assuming any liability for any claims, losses, or damages arising out of the use of this book. The reader should not rely on the author or publisher of this book for any professional advice.

Prices, commissions, fees, and other costs mentioned in the text or shown in samples in this book probably do not reflect real costs where you live. Inflation and other factors, including geography, can cause the costs you might encounter to be much higher or even much lower than those we show. The dollar amounts shown are simply intended as representative examples.

Acknowledgments

Thanking people is always tricky, as you really don't want to leave anyone out. So on that note, I'd like to give an all-encompassing thank-you to my family and friends. You know who you are. In particular, though, I'd like to thank my mom, who worked as hard as anyone I've ever known to keep a roof over our heads while I was growing up. You ran a real home-based business, Mom, and you didn't even know it.

Thanks need to go out to Richard Day, who got this book project rolling, and to editors Barbara Kuhne and Grace Yaginuma, who had the unenviable task of fixing my (many) mistakes and turning my words into a real book. In addition, I want to thank Norman Katz of Katzscan. Norman is an e-commerce consultant who actually got me started in my current home-based business by searching online and reaching out to me all those years ago. He remains both a colleague and a friend to this day.

Of course, I must reserve my biggest thanks for my wife, Maryellen. Not only is she the best wife a guy could hope for, but she's a true life partner in every sense of the term. I love you, sweets.

Lastly, I'd like to thank every boss who ever fired me.

Introduction

You — owning a home-based business? Sure, why not? In fact, welcome to the club!

Let me be one of the first to congratulate you. You are probably very excited over this decision, and perhaps even a little bit scared. Don't worry; being scared is perfectly normal, so let me just reassure you: *Yes, you can do this.* With some guidance, good advice, and hard work, you will be well on your way to successfully being self-employed in a home-based business.

And trust me, being self-employed in a real home-based business is the greatest feeling in the world. The benefits include the following:

- You make the rules (ice cream at noon!).

- You set your work schedule.

- You can bring your kids (or your pets) to work.

- You can spend more time with your family (or not; it's your choice).

- You can call your boss an idiot and get away with it.

- You can earn what you are truly worth, not what someone else thinks you are worth (and they never seem to think you are worth all that much, do they?). If you succeed, you will certainly earn more than you would at a regular job.

There is nothing like working for yourself. No successful home-based entrepreneur

I ever met would want to go back to a regular job. That should tell you something.

And no matter what type of home-based business you want to start, this book can really help you. It doesn't matter if you want to work from home using a computer; make a product and sell it; run a business servicing the local area (like a contractor, computer service professional, etc.); or you want to have a business *in* your home (like a daycare) — I can help you become successfully self-employed.

> **Running a successful home-based business is something you CAN do.**

The key is actually doing the *right* things and knowing *which* mistakes to avoid. This is where experience comes in. To be blunt, I failed in my first two home-based business attempts. Why did I fail? Because I did things that now seem so stupid that they astonish me. I made mistakes I'd never make now, because I now know better. And here's the funny thing — I see so many beginning home-based business owners make the *exact same mistakes*.

I wish somebody could have sat me down all those years ago and talked to me about the prices I was charging for my product. Or about how my invoicing practices were crippling me. Or how I needed to really focus on my business more and take it seriously. Oh, I *thought* I was serious, but in hindsight, I was about as serious and focused as four unemployed guys sitting in a garage saying, "Man, we should start a band" after draining the keg.

But I definitely learned from my mistakes, and today I run a full-time, successful home-based business that I started from scratch. I've operated all kinds of businesses: I've run a local professional service, I've sold a product from my home, and currently I work from home on my computer. I've failed, come back, and succeeded. Along the way, I've learned a lot of things. In fact, I learned just as much from my failures as I have from my successes.

And I've put everything I've learned into this book. *Start & Run a Real Home-Based Business* will help you by showing you both what to do and what *not* to do. If you're serious about owning a real home-based business, then this book is for you.

Tone and Structure of This Book

This is a different type of home-based business book than you may be used to. It's not a "lite" step-by-step guide filled with a lot of useless information. Instead, it's meant to focus on the things that will *really* matter to the success of your business.

To give you an example, I'm not going to spend 39 pages telling you all about office machines (you don't need a book to go over that, do you?). Instead, I'll do it in 39 sentences — well, less, actually. I'd much rather spend time talking about your invoicing or your pricing, which are far more important to your business success than which type of fax machine you buy (to be honest, you probably don't even need a fax machine).

This book is written in a "No BS" style. I'm going to come right out and say "here's what you must do," and I'll also tell you in no uncertain terms what things to avoid. Nothing is sugarcoated. So let me apologize in advance for what may seem like some stern advice. I'm not going to beat around the bush and give you warm and fuzzy "feel-good" information. I'm going to tell you straight up what has helped businesses succeed, and what has made them fail.

For example, I've read books about home-based businesses that suggest it is okay to make homemade flyers in the beginning and skip advertising because it's costly. That's pure BS. For most businesses, it's *not* okay to skip advertising, and homemade flyers are pretty close to useless.

I've brought together more than 50 topics that are essential to the success of any home-based business. Some of the topics are fundamental subjects that you'd expect, such as taxes, advertising, and the Internet. Others are things you've likely never thought of, such as how to get your spouse/partner on board, finding hidden niche markets, and when to drop trouble customers. Still others are vital to success but are things you usually don't find out about until after they hurt you — like how having a big customer can actually hurt you, and how to make sure you get paid.

Start & Run a Real Home-Based Business is more or less written from me to you. It does not assume that you're a big, rich business-person or a highly paid superexecutive. There are plenty of good business books out there written by successful, millionaire CEOs, but can you really relate to them on the scale of your home-based business? I certainly can't. Mention the word "capital" once, and you've lost me. See, I do not have, nor do I have access to, "capital."

A CEO regaling the reader with tales about what he or she did at the latest shareholder meeting to get people to see things his or her way isn't very helpful to a home-based business owner either. My "shareholders" consist of my wife and my two dogs — and trust me, they don't always see things my way. I'd include the cat, but she's fairly well above it all.

This book talks in plain language to people who want to start small businesses with limited amounts of money. Unlike many other business books, I won't tell the story about how "Donna from Wisconsin" took a risk, and with $85,000 opened a …

Listen, if you have $85,000 sitting around to risk, well, let's just say we're not playing the same game.

When I started, I didn't have $85,000 just lying around (I assume that would be the elusive "capital"). Donna's story is completely meaningless to me and anyone else who doesn't have that kind of money to burn. So I don't mention "capital" at all in this book.

The book consists of short, easy-to-read essays on various topics that are vital to a home-based business owner. Some of the topics are two pages long; others might fill five pages. The three major sections are **Mind**, **Body**, and **Soul**.

- **Mind** covers the entrepreneurial mindset — your attitude, motivation, beliefs, feelings, and emotions. Successfully running a home-based business is as much about attitude as it is about skill; this part addresses these topics.

- **Body** covers the nuts and bolts of your business. How much money you'll need to start; business cards; home offices; advertising; paperwork; computers; taxes; etc.

- **Soul** addresses the topics in between mind and body. How do you get your spouse on board with your idea? How much should you charge for your product or service? And also: dealing with troublesome clients; taking days off; your competition; etc.

I structured the book in this way for two reasons:

1. I love easy-to-read books that are chock-full of useful information. Books you can open to any page at any time and get something out of them. Don't you love those kinds of books too? That's the kind of book you're reading now.

2. I really want to cover a lot of information, and this is the best way to do it.

They say experience is the best teacher. Well, this book is entirely based on my real experience running home-based businesses.

Types of Businesses This Book Can Help

To explain what I mean by a real home-based business, it might be easier to start out with what I don't mean.

I'm *not* talking about a multilevel marketing "opportunity" where you sign up your friends to buy packets of green seaweed jelly cleverly marketed as health food (or as a hair product — I've seen it marketed both ways, which makes one wonder).

Nor am I talking about online "build a website and get rich quick" schemes, or anything you need to throw a "party" to sell. I'm also not talking about silly "work at home" schemes like stuffing envelopes, filling out surveys, or becoming a "mystery shopper." The only people who generally make money on schemes like that are the companies offering them to you, and also "Dave from California" who is in all the advertising testimonials from these companies.

And finally, I'm not talking about fluff business ideas such as "you can start a coupon clipping service, a shopping service, or a scrapbooking service." You *can* start such a service, but you'll soon find out that there's no money in coupons, and you'll go broke.

What I'm talking about is running a legitimate, professional business that is based in your home. Here is a small sampling of the businesses for which this book will be helpful:

- Home computer/professional services for which the world is your customer, such as medical billing, writing, web design, computer programming, market consulting, niche-market accounting, sales training, etc.

- Any of the building trades where you serve the local market, such as carpentry, plumbing, electrical work, painting, roofing, general handiwork, etc.

- Local professional services such as computer repair/networking, local advertising sales/consulting, wedding photography, accounting, etc.

- A business where you will make a product and sell it, either locally or internationally. For example, making a special kind of jewelry or a particular type of birdhouse, specializing in a certain type of painting, or offering frame-ready prints to the world via the Internet.

- Outdoor services such as landscaping, lawn mowing, or tree pruning.

- Local services such as pet sitting, house/office cleaning, home health care, home inspection, pest control, DJ services, kids entertainment at parties, etc.

- Services based *in* your home, like a home daycare, music lessons, hair styling, portrait photography, etc.

- Apart from these and many other businesses for which this book is relevant, many "semi-entrepreneurial" professionals like realtors and car salespeople will also find this book very useful. I refer to these occupations as semi-entrepreneurial because the people in these lines of work often rely somewhat on the companies they are affiliated with to provide many of their customers/clients. However, they are also very entrepreneurial in the sense that the company may only provide a desk and some advertising, and the rest is up to them.

This book makes for a great companion to all the other Self-Counsel Press "Start & Run" books. If there's one for your particular business, buy that book too. Your chances of making it will be that much better.

A Few Points to Keep in Mind

1. Disclaimer

The advice in this book is given with the best of intentions to help you succeed in business. However, I am not a lawyer, and I have no magic powers either. In other words, I cannot guarantee you any level of success. So if you bought this book hoping it would help "Dave's Lint Recycling" take off, and you fail, don't blame me or my publisher.

I repeatedly stress using the services of professionals in this book. Lawyers, accountants, advertisers, and web designers are all out there, and they can all help you. I'll give you some general advice on a topic such as taxes, but your accountant trumps what I say, so trust him or her.

2. I do not like statistics, and I use very few

I do not employ many statistics in this book. The most I'll do is state something very general, like "90 percent of the time, that won't work." I do this for two reasons:

a) Most "stats" are simply made up by the people claiming whatever it is they are claiming.

b) Statistics used to make a point are very subjective. Two people arguing over whether second-hand smoke is harmful or not can both cite lots of statistics that back their viewpoints. People like "hiding" behind statistics; I choose not to.

3. **You're going to have to get your hands dirty**

There are some people out there who want everything done for them, or want to start a business without learning anything new. I've seen advertisements such as "Internet business in a box" sold on TV, with the tagline "you don't need to know anything about the Internet!"

I'm sorry, you can't run a home-based Internet business without knowing anything about the Internet. I'm not saying you have to be an IT guru or a webmaster, but if you want to have an Internet business, you're going to have to (*gasp*) learn a little bit about the Internet.

So you *are* going to have to get your hands dirty — no matter what it is you want to do. This means doing some reading, and learning new things.

There are places in this book where I'll talk about accepting credit cards or getting a website domain name. I'll tell you in general terms where you need to go for such information, but I'm going to leave it up to you to actually do it and set up an account. This is for two reasons:

a) If I held your hand the whole way, this book would be thousands of pages long.

b) To succeed in a home-based business, you have to do these things yourself. It's like learning to drive — sooner or later, you're going to have to take the wheel.

4. **Enjoy yourself**

This book was a joy to write, and I truly hope you enjoy reading it. Indeed, I tried to make it as fun as possible. So get ready, open your mind, and let's go.

Part 1
MIND

Chapter 1

A LITTLE CREDIBILITY: HOME-BASED BUSINESSES I HAVE RUN

Since I'm going to give you a lot of advice regarding business, it's only fair that you know my credentials, so I'll lay them out for you right here in the beginning.

I currently work for myself, from my home, doing "real" work. My home-based business is a professional writing and small-business consulting service. Companies from all over the world hire me to do all kinds of writing and marketing projects for them: brochures, sales proposals, websites, press releases, etc. I developed this business from the ground up. Last year, from my basement office, I earned in the low six figures.

I'd like to stress that I have no special training or college degree — I'm simply someone who writes well. The difference between me and many other people who write well is that I know how to turn my skill into a business.

Before my writing business, I ran another successful computer-based business from my home — freelance programming. I also successfully sold a product from my home, and in the 1990s, I ran two advertising/direct mail businesses where I serviced the local area. These two advertising businesses I eventually failed in, which is important in the big scheme of things.

So I've had experience in almost all aspects of a home-based business — I've run a business where I was based at home, but serviced the local area; I've made a product in my home and sold it; and I currently work from home on my computer, servicing the entire world via the Internet. I started with nothing, and have experienced both failure and success.

Here are more detailed descriptions of my entrepreneurial experiences (for those who are interested).

1992–1994: Intriguing Ideas

My first home-based business was an advertising/marketing business that I started when I was in my early twenties. It was named Intriguing Ideas. I quit a good job and dove in full time. Mainly I created and sold my own direct mail coupons door-to-door to local businesses (essentially, I competed with Money Mailer and Valpak). I also did some advertising/marketing consulting work for local businesses (many that were home based). I was pretty good at this part — I made a lot of other businesses money. I've always been good at that. Too bad I made some big mistakes in my *own* business. I eventually went broke and had to get a job again (and again, and again — I tend to get fired a lot). Throughout this book, I talk about this first business often, and tell you about the mistakes I made so you don't repeat them. If I knew then what I know now, that business would have made it.

1995–1996: Night Owl Marketing

A bit later, I sold ads and built websites for local businesses for a very young World Wide Web, and I also did computer repair work. I made a few more mistakes, and the Internet was still too young to make a real living selling ads on it. While I was a little more successful here than my first time around, I still could not quite make a living,

and had to go back to a job (and we know how that will end).

2001–2004: Night Owl e-Ventures

After being fired again (gee, there's a surprise), I used my computer skills and started a home-computer programming business utilizing a specific type of software I was proficient in. Finally, I had learned the right things to do, and this home-based business turned out to be a success. For a few years, I made a nice living working out of my house (about $40k to $60k per year). However, there was a small flaw — the specific software that I was proficient in was being phased out by the company that made it — which would make me obsolete. I knew I had to do something else.

2004: Favorite Clubs (Under Night Owl e-Ventures)

Branching out from computer-related work, I then decided to try my hand at selling a product. I made golf clubs in my garage and sold them online. I did well, but my garage was really too small for this type of operation — inventory became a real problem. I pulled the plug rather than address that issue, but I have no doubt I could have made a decent living doing this, as I had become very proficient at marketing a business both online and off.

2004–Present: Night Owl e-Ventures Inc. ("Inc." Added in 2004)

So in the wake of not wanting to make golf clubs in my small garage, I finally followed my heart and decided to start a writing business. I love to write and had been told I was a good writer all my life. In addition, in every job I ever had, this skill was recognized and I was asked to write. I'd write marketing literature, newsletters, sales pieces, press releases — you name it. So I figured since I'd been unofficially doing business writing for years, I might as well try to get paid for it. Writing turned out to be right for me, and so business has succeeded. Now I write full time, and I couldn't be happier.

In addition to these businesses, I have provided consulting services to small and home-based businesses for years. I've also sold advertising to small and home-based businesses, helped them grow by devising marketing strategies, and generally been involved in making all kinds of businesses succeed for the past 20 years.

I never set out to be Donald Trump (I have better hair). Nor do I want to make tens of millions of dollars or run a huge company. All I want is to make a nice, quiet, anonymous living from the comfort of my home. I want to do work that pleases me, and I want to be paid well for it. I also want the time and freedom to enjoy my life.

I'm doing what millions of people dream of doing — working for myself at home and making a nice full-time living.

I'm doing that right now, and I can help you do it too.

Chapter 2

THE NEW BUSINESS BLINDERS

To me, being an entrepreneur and owning a home-based business are more about mind-set than anything else. In our "go to school then get a good job" culture, it takes a very special person to even *think* about going it alone. So you are to be commended for even reading this book. You are way ahead of most people in terms of motivation and ambition.

However, motivation and ambition are not enough. Not by a long shot.

In fact, in many ways, motivation and ambition can *hurt* a home-based business owner. This is because of a phenomenon I like to call the New Business Blinders. I want to discuss this right here in the beginning, because you'll see the term crop up again in the pages that follow.

The New Business Blinders are usually donned within a few weeks after making the decision to start a business. Once you reach the point of no return — the point where you decide that yes, you are going to start a home-based business — an order is put in for your blinders. You don't need to do anything — the thoroughly evil Department of Business Failures handles this for you (how nice of them!). All you have to do is wait for your pair of blinders to show up, which is usually a short time after you have the initial details of your home-based business worked out.

And trust me, they'll be a perfect fit — unlike airline seats, one size truly does fit all.

And they are so comfortable, you won't want to remove them. They start working right away, but the minute you envision yourself and your home-based business succeeding is when the blinders really kick in.

So, what do these blinders do (besides giving me a clever metaphor to write about)? Well, they do exactly what you think they do — they blind you to the obvious. Fueled by your motivation, hopes, dreams, and ambitions, your shiny New Business Blinders completely shut you off from logic and reason. And they do it without you noticing.

You may not be old enough to remember *I Love Lucy* — well, neither am I really, but during the '70s, it was on every weekday afternoon, which meant a child staying home from school could catch an episode. Since missing school was a popular pastime of mine, I am fairly familiar with the adventures of Lucy and Ethel. In one episode, Lucy and Ethel make and sell salad dressing. Hilarity ensues until Ricky does some basic math and finds out the girls are actually *losing* money on each jar. This is funny not only because of Lucy and Ethel's solution (pretend the dressing is poison so people cancel their orders), but because their experience is so common. Not the poison part (even *pretending* to poison your customers is really bad for public relations, and not recommended), but the losing money part.

It happens all the time — people start home-based businesses that actually *lose* money. They do this because they fail to take into account many of the expenses involved. The New Business Blinders are responsible for this.

For example, in my first business, I sold a direct-mail coupon package. My "blinder moment" was when I failed to get an exact price for postage based on a prototype. My printer used a fairly heavy paper stock for the coupons (I didn't even think of paper stock and weight, which was a huge error on my part). This doubled my postage cost over what I had anticipated. On 10,000 pieces, this cost turned out to be very, very high.

My New Business Blinders were working quite well.

I thought I was doing everything right — I was concerned about printing costs, first-class versus third-class postage, envelope stuffing costs, getting a shiny new computer (which was a big deal in 1992), making the coupons, selling them, etc. I even thought about the future, how my partner Jim and I would franchise our business model to other entrepreneurs and rule over a vast empire of direct-mail coupon businesses, which, now that I think about it, is almost absurd. Essentially, my goal was to be "King of the Free Pizza Coupons," which sounds like something you'd dream about after eating too much candy.

But in my zeal to storm the gates and crush the direct-mail competition, I neglected to make a *real* prototype out of *actual* materials and see what the costs would be. I just didn't see the point in doing so. Dumb. And all too common.

And, unlike Lucy, this wasn't a hijinks jam that could be worked out in a half an hour. This was real, and I was in trouble. I essentially had to raise my price substantially in midcampaign. This meant that some people got my product at one price; others paid more. This angered some people when they found out. Oops.

New Business Blinders do this. They cause you to ignore the obvious and see past the unpleasant.

The blinders are not just cost related, either. Suppose you want to build a product and sell it. It's not fun to think about "where will I get my materials, and what happens if that source dries up?" It's *much* more fun to fantasize about shaking hands on a million dollar deal and getting fitted for a beach chair in Aruba.

Or if you want to have a pet-sitting service, it's no fun to think about what you will do if you show up and the dog is ill (or is menacing toward you). Or if the puppy bursts out and runs away when you first open the door. These are things that could drastically affect your business, and you have to think about (and prepare for) them.

Sometimes, our overwhelming desire to succeed makes us ignore the pitfalls that could occur.

New Business Blinders come standard with *every single business;* however, their power fades over time. They are easily the strongest with your first business. In subsequent businesses (or with time spent in your first business), they are less and less powerful, eventually reaching the level of effectiveness of Dollar Store sunglasses. But you always have to be aware of them. They feed on your ambition and your desire to succeed, and they will always be present.

Parts of this book (especially the "Mind" section) are spent pointing out the things that your New Business Blinders will prevent you from seeing. So if something seems obvious to you, I mention it because of my experience with the New Business Blinders.

Chapter 3

STARTING AND NAMING YOUR BUSINESS

The first thing I'm going to tell you is to go start your home-based business. Really — if you don't go out and actually start a business, nothing further will happen. If you have already started a business, read this part anyway, as it'll probably be helpful.

What Type of Business to Start?

For the purposes of this book, I am going to assume you will be starting a simple sole-proprietor business.

There are several different business structures, such as corporations, LLCs, and partnerships, but your typical small, home-based business will likely start as a sole proprietorship (or DBA, which means "Doing Business As").

You *can* start a corporation or LLC if you want to, but for most people, it's a daunting thing to do, and usually a roadblock to progress. Although I myself am now incorporated, I did not do so until 2004, several years into my current business. I know if I had tried to form a corporation right out of the gate, I likely never would have done it. There are boring legalities to investigate, forms to complete, searches for similar names, lawyers to hire, etc. Compare this to starting a sole proprietorship: one quick form to fill out, a few bucks to pay, and I was done. Elapsed time: 15 minutes.

The choice was pretty easy for me. And when the time did come to incorporate, my wife volunteered to do it, much to my relief. (All I had to do was sign what she put in

9

front of me, which I always immediately do. She could put a document that ruins my life in front of me, and I'll happily sign it.)

So if forming a corporation seems daunting to you, forget about it for now and just start a sole proprietorship. You can worry about incorporating later when you actually make money. If you are concerned about the liability protection a corporation gives, you can always ask a lawyer for advice.

Some of you may want to start a partnership — which is the same as a DBA except there are two or more people — but I do not recommend that. (Read more on partnerships in Chapter 4.)

Avoid Meaningless Roadblocks

I'm also going to advise you to avoid meaningless roadblocks and not get caught up in things that don't really matter. Let me illustrate this point with a brief story. I have a friend who recently wanted some advice about starting a business. She wanted to actually run two companies that were intertwined, with one being a nonprofit entity donating money to a particular cause.

She was concerned about how to set this all up: What are the rules regarding a nonprofit? How would it be structured? How should she put the donation aspect in her marketing? How would she determine which entity would get the lion's share of the money? How much should she donate?

Essentially, my one comment was: "Why don't you go make some money first, *then* worry about how to divvy it up?"

Really, it was that simple. Why worry about *how* you are going to donate the profits before you even make one sale? She hadn't even made a prototype of her product yet, and she was worrying about how to donate the nonexistent profits.

I tell this story not to make my friend feel bad, but to illustrate something that is *very* common with people who are starting a business. I did the same thing years ago in my first business. I was worried about how much commission I was going to pay my salespeople and how I would word a noncompete agreement. This was before I made a single sale on my own — I didn't have any sales to pay commission *on*, yet I was worried about how much I was going to pay my future sales force. This was a roadblock that served no logical purpose. Don't worry about the money until you actually *make* some. Paying a lawyer to form a corporation is a bridge you can (and perhaps should) cross later on, but at the beginning, before you've made a single dollar, it's a meaningless worry.

So go start your business. It's very easy to do. Pick a name. Go to your local county building (or in Canada, your CRA office) with some ID, fill out a simple form, and pay the fee. That's all you need to do to get started. This can also be done easily online.

The business you start won't change your life *at all* unless you do something with it. In other words, you can start it, and if you never do anything with it, well, so be it. Nobody will call you, and no men in dark suits will come to your house and make you do push-ups or anything like that. So you have nothing to lose by starting it.

I want you to start it because in order to succeed, you actually have to *do* something. Starting your business is that little step that puts you ahead of 99 percent of people who are all talk and no action.

Select a Business Name

Naming a business is one of those psychological roadblocks that prevents many people from starting in the first place. They hem and haw trying to find the perfect name. They ask family and friends. They design endless logos on the computer. They go over all kinds of names in their heads ... *"Bill's bug killing"? No ... "Bill the bugman"? No ... "Buggy Bill blasts the belligerent black bugs back into the big blue—" No ...*

If you can't come up with anything, use your initials or your name. If your name is John Smith, call it JS Enterprises, or Smith Technology, or JS Tech, or something similar. And don't worry if someone else in the country has the same business name — chances are, they do (how many Tony's Pizzas do you think there are?). It's likely only your local area that you have to worry about, and the people who help you register your business will let you know if your name is okay.

What I'm trying to stress to you is *do not let the name stand in your way.* Since starting a business is so easy and inexpensive, if you come up with a better name later, you can easily go file that one. For now, get started.

Try not to let your business name pigeonhole you. That's why a nice generic name is best. Naming your business Bill's Slug Removal pretty much limits you to removing slugs. If someone wants to have bees or ants removed, they likely won't call you, even if you *do* remove bees and ants.

Bill's Pest Services is a much better name. Then, be it slugs, bees, or even stinkbugs, you're covered.

Also, don't worry too much about an Internet domain name for your business. If you can get www.billspestservices.com, great (just go to register.com or godaddy .com to check and buy domain names). But if your preferred name is already taken, other superb Internet names are *always* available. You just have to get creative. For example, if you are starting a pest service in Florida, how about www.ikillfloridabugs .com? Or www.floridabugkiller.com? When it comes to an online name, the cleverer it is, the better. Creative, witty, easy-to-remember names like this are always available, and can be had dirt cheap. Just use your imagination.

The important thing is to pick a name and start your business.

Open a Business Bank Account

On your way home from starting the business, go open a checking account for it. This is another vital step, both for tax reasons and for psychological reasons. Having a bank account for your business makes it seem like you *truly* are in business.

Again, nothing has to happen with this account. If you don't do any business, your account can just sit there, but having business checks with your company name on them is very uplifting in a motivational sense, and I feel it's a very important step.

Once you get the business started, the bank account opened, and an Internet domain name secured, you are ready to go. Scared? Don't be. While it's true that it can be a very trying ride at times, trust me when I tell you there is nothing like owning your own home-based business. It's the best feeling in the world.

Which you'll soon know firsthand.

Chapter 4

PARTNERSHIPS ARE USUALLY A BAD IDEA: HERE'S WHY

Ahh, the partnership. That type of business where two friends or family members decide to take on the world side by side. Started with the best of intentions, and with the duties clearly spelled out and divvied up ("Jen will do the business stuff; I'll do the sales"), partnerships almost always end badly.

I won't beat around the bush. I think the underlying reason why most partnerships fail is the *true* reason they are usually formed in the first place: Nobody wants to go it alone. I put "true" in italics because nobody will really admit to this. People say other things, like, "I'm the idea person and she is the production person," or "I'll do the selling and he'll do the books."

But the real reason they are going into a partnership is that they are simply scared and want someone else to lean on (or go down the drain with). And you know, I can definitely see the attraction in partnering up. It's simple, really: Would you rather explore a spooky house alone or with a friend? Well, business is like a spooky house. Having someone there with you is definitely attractive. I did this in my first business, so I understand the allure.

However, let's not pretend: A partnership that starts because "two is better than one" gets everything off on the wrong foot. It's definitely a problem if the partners are in business because they *feel* better together, not because they *work* better together.

Now that I've identified the primary reason why most partnerships are formed in the first place, let's look at a few problems-in-waiting in many partnerships.

Unequal Roles/Limited Skills

When two partners do not have clearly defined skills, often one partner will do the more glamorous work and the other partner will be in a lesser role. Nothing as blatant as "I'll come up with the ideas, and you can clean up the worms"; more along the lines of "I'll do the marketing/selling, and you can do the paperwork."

This usually happens because one partner is, for some reason, deemed "better" at something than the other. Unless one person is *clearly* better (as in being a professional), this usually will cause problems. I'll accept the fact that my accountant knows more about taxes and accounting than I do. If we ever become partners, the taxes and books are his by default. I'm sure he'll agree. But if I started a partnership with a neighbor, I shouldn't have to do the books because I "know computers better." That will eventually cause problems.

To further illustrate this, let's say two people named Marie and Dina are going into business. Marie says Dina should do the paperwork, "Because she's good at it and I'm not. I'm more of a bubbly people person." And Dina agrees — Marie couldn't even *spell* "taxes," never mind do anything more than basic math. So she'll do the paperwork, and Marie will get the accounts.

But trust me, unless Dina really, *really* loves doing paperwork, there will be trouble.

Oh she'll do it, but over time, she'll begin to resent it. Because she didn't get into this partnership to do only this kind of work while Marie gets to ignore it completely. Again, the disclaimer here is that if Dina is already an accountant, this division of work is fine. If she loves doing paperwork (like my wife does … or so she tells me), things will be fine.

But assuming she doesn't dream about doing paperwork, she will take exception to having to do it day after day. And that resentment will build. It will probably fester until one day, after an all-night session fixing Marie's "cute guy discount," Dina grabs a (sharp) pen and …

Okay, never mind what happens then. You get the point (as did Marie).

So unless you are both *completely* okay with one partner being a little more dominant, or doing the more "glamorous" work, beware. This leads us to the second problem …

One Partner Is Simply Better Than the Other

I'll be blunt: I wouldn't make the greatest business partner for most people in a small business. (However, international corporations wanting to explore seven-figure marketing deals, please feel free to call.) In a nutshell, I'd have a pretty bad attitude, because I would expect my partner to be *just as focused as I am*. If you aren't, and you're my partner, there will be friction. And I'm pretty well focused on business these days.

This happens all the time in partnerships. One partner is usually more "into it" than the other. This breeds resentment, and it's the beginning of the end. Both partners have to have the same mindset regarding skill, work ethic, motivation, drive, etc.

Another example of an unequal partnership is one formed with a "hanger-on." A hanger-on is a friend/family member/ acquaintance who wants in on your business when you tell him or her about your plans. Such people know that by hitching their wagon to you, they have a shot at doing something they could not do on their own. They want to be a part of your success, and don't want to be left behind.

Beware of this. Such partners are anchors waiting to drag you down. *I'll be honest: If neither of you can run a business on your own, it's probably not a good idea to partner up*. So cut loose the hanger-on.

Friends and Family Members in Business

Another reason partnerships fail is because being in business with friends or family members is a very difficult thing for most people to pull off. Many partnerships are formed by two (or more) friends who decide to go into some sort of business together. The "not going it alone/feel good" motivation is strong here, and because the people are friends, they assume they will be able to resolve just about any issue. Well, that never happens. Here's why: Money and work change everything.

They say, "Don't loan money to friends." They also say, "Don't hire friends." There are good reasons for these sayings: money, work, and friendships do not mix. It's easy to plot out your partnership when you are broke and in the planning stages. When there's nothing at stake, everything is easy. But what happens when the business starts to grow? Once decent sums of money (or debt) are involved, opinions will always differ, and being friends makes it harder to lay everything out on the table.

I had bosses that were not shy at all about telling me what they thought of me (it was never good). It was simple for them — they were my bosses, not my friends (thank God). But try telling your friends they aren't pulling their weight. Or their brochure design is lousy. Or they blew a big sale because of their personal problems. Or a million other little things. It's not so easy. And problems that fester will start to eat away at any business. This happened in my first business — I felt like I did all the work. I'll bet Jim felt that way too.

Partnerships That Can Work

Okay, now that I've basically doomed 90 percent of all partnerships, here are a few situations where they *can* work.

One partner has money, and will mostly remain silent

If one partner provides funding and understands this is an investment and not a guarantee, a partnership of this nature might work. This is more of a business relationship than "friends in business together" (which almost never works). The "money" partner can be involved in big decisions, but leaves the day-to-day running of the business to the other partner.

There is a *true* division of clearly defined skills

A computer programmer who gets together with an artist and a writer to create a video game is a good example of a meeting of the minds where everyone brings different, vital skills to the table. An accountant/business manager teaming up with a skilled mechanic to open an auto repair business is another. But for this to work, everyone has to have *true* skills, not the vague "I'm more creative, so I'll do the marketing."

Two professionals passionate about their work get together

When I say professionals, I mean people truly passionate about what they do. I mean two computer programmers working nights developing a new program, not only because they want to be in business, but because they love programming. I'm talking Bill Gates and Paul Allen, for example. I am *not* talking about an assistant manager of a greeting card store and a laid-off welder who say they are passionate about fixing cars. If they are so passionate about it, why weren't they doing it before? I'll bet 99 times out of 100 that last example is doomed to fail.

Husband and wife

For some couples, a business partnership can work rather nicely. If the marriage is strong, it's already a partnership. If you can make money together as well, all the better. In my business, I am the primary worker and my wife handles all the administrative work. While we're not officially a partnership (we're a corporation now), it works very well for us.

So to repeat, my advice is to forget about forming a partnership unless it fits into one of the four preceding categories. However, I realize the "not going it alone" motivation is *very* strong, so if you *must* have a partnership, do yourself a favor and go to a lawyer and have him or her help you draft an agreement. Spell out duties, expenses, division of assets, etc. You'll be better off in the long run.

Chapter 5

FORGET THE BUSINESS PLAN … BUT PLAN FOR YOUR BUSINESS

If you start a business, invariably the topic of the *business plan* will come up. Be it a relative, a business consultant, a banker … at some point, somebody will ask you, "Can I see your business plan?" They ask this in the same accusing tone that a 1980s border guard would use when asking for your identification papers as you tried to leave East Germany. It's enough to make you literally squirm with discomfort.

For the record, a business plan is a fairly detailed and complicated document of significant length that states what your business is, what it will do, who it will sell to, who needs your product/service, etc.

A business plan serves three functions:

1. *It's used in order to get financed by a bank or venture capitalist.* (However, as I will point out in Chapter 22, you aren't getting any outside money for your home-based business.)

2. *It makes you think about your business.* Wise old men will nod their heads and say this part is vital. I don't need to tell you that. Instead, I'll assume that you've already given this some thought. More on this in a second …

3. *It serves as a* huge *roadblock to actually doing anything.* How big of a roadblock is it? Well, remember that nine-page research report you had to do for midterm? Remember how you put it off, and instead went

down to the lake with the gang and got caught by the school attendance police? The reason you put it off is because research reports, especially the nine-page variety, are HORRIBLY PAINFUL AND UNPLEASANT TO WRITE.

My point is, a business plan is ten times as unpleasant to write, and you do not have the looming presence of a rather sneaky attendance person prodding you on. So in reality, *you can put off doing a business plan forever.* Which is what happens to most people.

So I say don't worry about a business plan at the outset — you don't need one. Not now, anyway.

> **Not doing a business plan does not mean you do not have to plan for your business!**

There are countless business consultants out there who will tell you different. Oddly, many will offer assistance in writing your business plan (for a fee, of course). There are also plenty of guides and pieces of software that will help you write your business plan. However, in my opinion, they are a waste of money.

I say this because I'm a successful businessperson and I've never written a business plan. (I *have* put one off. I'll get to it someday, when business slows down.) I also know plenty of other successful businesspeople who never wrote a business plan either. So these business consultants can go back to doing what they do best (nothing), and leave the real-world advice to people actually doing real work.

Your Plan for Business

Starting and running a business is not something that should be taken lightly. So since I'm telling you to skip the business plan, it's only fair that I help you assess the viability of your business/idea by asking a few questions.

You should be able to answer all of these questions in detail. I'll explain why each is important. You can use the Your Plan for Business worksheet on the CD-ROM that accompanies this book to record your answers.

1. **What type of product/service will you provide? Explain in fifteen words or less.**

   If you cannot explain your overall concept or type of business in fifteen words or less, it's likely too complicated for your customers, and you probably don't have the proper focus. I can say I run a "professional business writing service." If your answer is, "well, we're going to make custom embroidered leather dog collars and also open up an art and crafts school for kids and moms every other Saturday and maybe even do some daycare on the side," you should probably tighten your focus a bit.

2. **Exactly who is your market?**

   You need to know exactly where your customers will be coming from. This sounds basic, but people start businesses all the time without knowing who their clients will be or where they will come from.

3. **How will people find out about your business? Be specific.**

Do you have any kind of plan to get the word out? You should.

4. **Is there a market for your business? Explain how you arrived at your answer.**

This is a hard question for many people to answer objectively. One way to see if there is a market is to check on the competition. Competition means there *definitely* is a market (and that's good). *No competition* may not necessarily mean there is no market, but if nobody else in your area is doing what you want to do, there may be a reason for that. For example, opening a skateboard repair service in a senior citizen retirement community might be a bad idea.

5. **What will set you apart from your competition?**

If you mention "price" in this answer, you may be in for a rough ride. If you say "better service," is that really true? What makes your service better? You can't say vague things like, "I'll do anything to make a customer happy." You should be able to answer *precisely* what will make your service better, and understand why your competition doesn't provide the same level of service.

In all honesty, sometimes it is acceptable to answer that nothing will set you apart. For example, I know just about every town could use another good plumber.

6. **What will your overhead costs be? Include everything from materials and the phone bill, to gas for driving to sales calls and electricity for lights.**

Please don't say you'll have no overhead and can thus pass the savings on to your customer. This is code for "I'll work long and hard for little pay." Every business, even my little home office, has significant expenses and overhead. Think long and hard and write down every cost you can think of.

7. **How many hours per week are you willing to work? Can your business realistically be run while keeping these hours?**

Be realistic about how much you are willing to work. I know at this point in my life (I'm 40), I am generally not willing to work more than 50 hours a week. This doesn't mean that I won't pull the occasional long week (I do), and I work plenty of 10- to 12-hour days, but if my business is going to *require* that I work more than 50 hours a week on a consistent basis, I will close up shop and go get a regular job. I'm lucky, too — many small businesses require a lot more hours. Are you ready for that? Do not start your business thinking you'll work a 60-hour week to get by unless you *really want* to work a 60-hour week (and plenty of people do). I'm just telling you to be true to yourself here. Working more than you want to will get tiresome really fast.

8. **What are your income expectations/needs, and can your business meet them, based on your answers to the preceding seven questions?**

Owning your own business is a great way to get paid what you are really worth. So, how much is your work worth? And can your income expectations/needs be satisfied by the demand for your business and the hours you are willing to work? You'd be surprised how many people think $30 an hour is a lot until they realize that works out to $1,200 for a 40-hour week. So at that rate, you can't make $75k a year unless you work well over 40 hours a week. (And that's assuming you get paid for all the hours you work, which you don't when you run a business.)

There are plenty of other things to think about, but these eight basic questions will give you a good, clear idea if your home-based business will be viable.

Chapter 6

PSST — YOUR "BIG IDEA" IS COMPLETELY WORTHLESS

When I talk to people about business, sooner or later someone will mention that they have a great business idea that they are working on. Usually they won't say exactly what it is, for fear of someone stealing it. However, they are confident that the idea will fly — big time. They talk about patents, protecting their idea from imitators, and perhaps even selling their idea to a company.

Yes, they have it all worked out. Fame, fortune, and extreme wealth would be right around the corner, except for one tiny detail: Nobody buys ideas.

Customers don't buy ideas, and businesses don't buy ideas. It's because ideas, in and of themselves, are completely worthless. It's the *end result* of the idea that is worth

something — either an actual new product, or a working business model.

Let me go over a few truths about ideas.

Somebody Else Has Likely Already Thought of Your Idea

I remember a friend of mine who had an idea for a child safety product. He was guarded about the details of this idea, but talked about it constantly in general terms. I finally pried out of him what it was, and I suggested we take a trip to the hardware store. Bam, there was his "big idea," right on the shelf, for $4.99.

My point is, no matter what it is you've thought of, the chances that someone else thought of the very same thing are extremely good. So before you head to the patent office, make sure your big idea isn't currently being manufactured by nine-year-olds in China.

Nobody Buys Ideas

I don't know of any company that buys ideas from people. So this whole dream of you selling this wonderful idea is just that — a dream. Ideas are a dime a dozen — *everyone* has a clever business idea in them.

What possibly can be sold is the actual fruition of an idea. Or the execution of it. In other words, if you have an idea for a product, well, you're going to have to make the product. Or, at the very least, come up with the exact technical details involved. Not general concepts like "I have an idea for a new door lock." You need to draw this lock in precise technical terms (not a notebook scribble), including a list of the needed materials. Then do a cost analysis of materials, assembly, etc. *Then* maybe you have something.

Better yet, just build the lock and shop it around.

This is the part that people trip on. They have great ideas, but when I ask deeper questions such as, "How long does it take to make?" and "Where will you get your materials, and how much will they cost?" the answers are vague. Those darn New Business Blinders are working again.

In order for your idea to be worth anything, you have to take it *beyond* the idea stage and start actually producing/planning — in detail — whatever your idea is. If you plan a product, you have to start producing

a real prototype. This may mean you have to do real research and/or work. For example, if your idea involves something being made out of plastic, well, you may have to find out how/where plastic molded items are produced, and how you can get yours made. Or where you can get the parts you need. The library and the Internet are your friends in this case.

To give you an example, when I was in my making-golf-clubs phase, I toyed with the idea of getting driver heads made with my brand name on them. I did some research and found several foundries in Taiwan that did exactly that. It took several hours of searching online, many emails, and a phone call or two in the middle of the night (so I could speak to someone during the day there), but I finally got what I wanted — a company willing to make my driver heads for roughly $10 each, with a reasonable minimum order (500 pieces). They sent me one generic club head to inspect, and I used it to build my prototype driver to see if I would be happy with it. (I was.)

All told, it took me maybe 40 hours of work to produce my prototype, and 39 of those hours were spent researching and finding the product.

It's the same if your idea is a service. In order for it to be worth anything, you'll have to start performing that service on a small scale.

Quite frankly, this "beyond the idea stage" takes a lot of work, which is why most ideas never go anywhere. Everyone can talk about it — few can really do it. So if you take the actual idea to the next level, you are WAY beyond almost everyone else.

But What about a Patent?

In general terms, you cannot patent an idea. If you could, we'd need a *much* bigger patent office. Now, I say "in general terms" because I know there are lawyers out there who will disagree and will happily sit down with you ($250 an hour, please) to discuss your idea. In fact, they'll discuss it for hours on end.

You can certainly try to apply for a patent for your idea, but in almost every case, you are going to have to do the "beyond the idea stage" step I outlined above (meaning figuring out the *details*). THEN you might have a shot at a patent. Again, it takes work (and getting a patent is a topic that can fill another book).

Nobody Is Going to Steal Your Idea

Because of what I outlined above, your idea is largely safe, even if your neighbor finds out about it. Let's be real: Your neighbors have trouble taking down their Christmas lights. It's unlikely they are going to start Miller Industries (assuming their name is Miller, of course) based on your idea.

The fear of someone stealing your idea is what keeps many an entrepreneur from doing anything more than dreaming. In my day, I've heard *plenty* of business ideas from various people. What follows are a few that never went anywhere.

The Outlet Protector

This is the child safety product I mentioned before. A friend of mine thought he had *the* big idea when he thought of a little plastic box that you put over your outlets to keep

your kids from fiddling with plugs. He was bummed when he saw the product on sale at the hardware store for less than five dollars.

The Pizza Cheese Stabilizer

About ten years ago, I was having a conversation with a friend about business. He confessed he had a great idea he was working on. When I pressed for what it was, he replied: "Okay, here it is: When you pick up a box of pizza, you usually put it on the seat of the car, right? And the car seat is not level, so the pizza leans backwards. And the hot cheese slides to one end of the pizza, making a mess. Don't you hate that?"

I didn't have much of a comment, because this was never a big problem for me. On the off chance this happened, I used a fork to redistribute the cheese to its proper balance upon returning home. Elapsed time: nine seconds. But apparently, for some people, uneven cheese is a HUGE issue. Huge enough to warrant a product.

So my friend told me about the handy dandy pizza-cheese stabilizer gizmo. How does it keep your pizza level on your car seat? I honestly don't know. What's it made out of? I honestly don't know. Neither does my friend who told me of this great idea. All he had was the idea — he had no clue what form the product would actually take. But it would level out your pizza, and was a surefire winner, if he could just make it and get it to market.

To the dismay of level cheese lovers everywhere, this product never seemed to go beyond the idea stage.

The Party Place Website

"I'm gonna have a website where people having parties can list their party, and people can pay to see where the parties are!" exclaimed my breathless, unemployed 32-year-old friend.

"What parties?" I asked.

"You know — parties!" he exclaimed excitedly.

"No, I don't know," I replied. "None of the parties I go to lend themselves to complete strangers checking a website to find out where they are held. So what kind of parties would advertise on your website?"

His face dropped. "Well, last night this dude said there was a party. I couldn't find it … so I thought, 'Wouldn't it be great if I could look it up on the Internet?'"

And that was the end of the conversation. Apparently, my friend thought there was this huge glut of keg parties begging to found by unemployed 32-year-olds who still use the word *dude* in conversation.

Chapter 7

MAKE SURE YOU CHOOSE A BUSINESS THAT IS REALLY FOR YOU

So, why do you want a home-based business? It's a valid question, and it deserves an honest answer. Because the reason you want a home-based business will go a long way in not only determining its success or failure, but it will also determine the direction your business takes.

There are a lot of reasons why people want to start a home-based business, and all of them are valid. The very fact that you have the entrepreneurial bug makes you a cut above everyone else in my book (and this *is* my book)!

However, keep in mind that your reason for starting the business should match the type of business you are starting and your

lifestyle. This can sometimes be tricky, and is something a lot of people overlook.

For example, if your primary reason for starting a home-based business is to be home with your preschool kids, you need to start a business that is conducive to preschool kids being around. In other words, don't start a business where you will have to spend a lot of time on conference calls with roomfuls of marketing people, or a business where you will have to go see clients on a continual basis. In the middle of a conversation, corporate clients and marketing people do *not* want to hear, "Not now, Mommy is busy. We'll play Choopa Chok later." Not that marketing people have anything against kids, but they likely don't want to turn over the fourth quarter spread-sheets to someone who plays Choopa Chok.

Let's look at another reason people start businesses — money. Lots of money. However, if your reason for starting a home-based business is to get rich, you need to pick a business that can reasonably grow beyond the work you can do on an hourly basis. For example, if you wanted to start a psychic readings business for your local area, or perhaps become a magician who performs at parties, well, *you* are essentially the business, and there are only so many hours in a day. Your income is, for all intents and purposes, capped at however many hours *you* wish to work. This is true for many types of businesses.

Now, this in itself isn't bad — a magician performing at parties and business conventions can make a fine living. But again, the overall income is limited by how many hours the magician is willing to perform.

I realize that any business can grow at the hands of a clever marketer, but some are easier to grow than others. And businesses where you work face to face (and especially one where *you* are the selling point) have a fairly limited scope in terms of expansion and increasing your income.

For my own business, I changed it from marketing myself as a writer to myself offering "writing services." This means I have other freelancers take on certain projects, and then I approve their work. Since I see nobody face to face, I just changed some wording on my website and hired another writer.

Consider Your Lifestyle

In choosing your business, you also need to consider your lifestyle and what you enjoy doing. Otherwise, there will be trouble later on.

Here are a few examples of businesses conflicting with lifestyles:

- Someone who really doesn't like working weekends opens a catering business.

- Someone who doesn't like working evenings starts a home computer repair business (evenings are when most clients will be home).

- Someone who others rely on for care and/or transportation starts a courier service where he or she would be needed to deliver important documents at a moment's notice.

The conflicts here may seem obvious, but in the excitement of starting a business, the obvious often gets overlooked because of the New Business Blinders.

My first business was an advertising business where the main product was a direct-mail coupon. My business partner and I were *so* excited at the prospect of the direct-mail fortunes we'd make that we overlooked one teeny little thing — I *hated* to cold-call and sell door-to-door (and he worked full time, so he couldn't do it either). Well, cold-calling businesses and approaching them door-to-door are the primary ways a local direct-mail product is sold. Especially in the beginning.

Yeah, it should have been obvious to us. But it wasn't. Starting entrepreneurs are blind to a lot of obvious things. It wasn't until after all the planning was done and I had to hit the pavement and walked into that first business that I realized, "Wait a minute — I HATE doing this."

It was a horrible feeling. That first day, before that first sales call, I sat in my car for an hour and listened to Iron Butterfly's "In-A-Gadda-Da-Vida" over and over again, afraid to get out of the car. Talk about a pathetic sight. My business was doomed right then and there. I eventually forced myself to make sales calls (and even made some sales), but I hated every second of it. And the business slowly died.

That's why I'm telling you this now: No matter what business you are going into, make sure the business you pick *really* matches your goals, your lifestyle, your tolerance for work, your income expectations, etc. You'll be much better off in the long run.

Chapter 8

TEN REALLY GREAT THINGS ABOUT A HOME-BASED BUSINESS

In this book I go over a ton of things that will go wrong and point out important aspects of owning a business that you might miss. Essentially, I go over all sorts of "bad" things that could happen. So this chapter addresses only the good parts about owning a home-based business. It's my attempt to spread a little sunshine. With that in mind, here are ten great things about owning a home-based business.

1. You Are Paid What You Are Really Worth

Do you think your work and efforts are worth $95 per hour, but your employer begs to differ? Well, once you *are* the employer, you set the rate. No more feeling underpaid — if you feel underpaid in your own business, trust me, you're doing something wrong.

2. You Call the Shots. All of Them

You set the work rules, the hours of operation, the amount that gets spent on advertising — you do it all. Everything is run your way. For many people (myself included), this is a big deal. See, I always thought I could do it better than management — and now I get to do just that.

You also get to largely pick and choose the work you want to do. If you want to specialize in the one or two aspects of your business that really interest you, you can. Nobody is going to give you projects you don't like — you have complete control over accepting them or not.

3. The Commute Is Usually Really Nice

My commute is about 50 feet. As long as I successfully navigate the sleeping cat on the stairs, there's very little traffic. Depending on the type of home-based business you choose to start, this could vary, but in most cases, your driving/commuting time will go down.

4. More Time at Home

I suppose this could be a good or bad thing depending on your home life, but I'm fairly confident that most people who start a home-based business partly do it so they can spend more time with their families. The absence of a long commute and the fact that you set the hours you work means more time at home.

5. You Get to See More of Your Children's Activities

One of the biggest complaints many working parents have is that they miss a lot of school plays, concerts, little league games, etc. Working for yourself in a home-based business means you can attend more of these activities. I realize this could mean attending a three-hour play where your child has a 30-second, nonspeaking part playing a tree; or you being witness to yet another 23-0 error-filled thrashing that is called in the second inning due to the mercy rule, but *at least you were there.*

6. You Get Out of Doing Things You Don't Want to Do

This is the flip side to having more free time. The nature of a home-based business is such that vitally important work can spring up at *any* time. Meaning it's the perfect excuse to get out of doing things you don't want to do.

I'm serious — this is a benefit of owning your own business. How many times have you fumbled for an excuse *not* to do something? Your own business is a slam-dunk excuse that nobody can argue with.

This excuse works almost universally. Say you have a neighbor who invites you to his annual BBQ, which is something you'd be happy to attend if it weren't for the lousy food, your neighbor's questionable hygiene, the three free-roaming dogs he insists on keeping, and the pool that doubles as a … well, let's not get gross, but last year, there were 11 small children swimming for five hours with no bathroom breaks.

Instead of damaging relations with this key figure in your life, you can instead just tell your neighbor that you have an important client (Mr. Recliner) that needs attention.

I know it sounds like I'm kidding, but I'm not. The simple fact is that working for yourself gives you a "get out of stuff free" card. It's a nice perk.

7. No Coworkers

This can be a double-edged sword. The upside is coworkers are usually in the way — in the way of your career, in the way of getting things accomplished, in the way when you have a great idea …

However, I do admit that sometimes there's a slight bit of isolation in working in a home-based business. I did like many of the people I worked with, and I miss the camaraderie. If you're a big "people person" and like coworkers a lot, make sure you're okay with the fact that there are none in your own business (at least not initially).

In the end, I'm a bit of a loner, and I prefer the company of my two dogs and one cat, who make ideal coworkers. No back-stabbing, no office politics — just give them a meal and they're happy.

8. You Can Do Usual "Weekend" Things When You Wish

Do you know what stores look like on Tuesday afternoon? They're empty. People who work normal business hours have no idea how nice it is to go shopping when there aren't crowds of people and long lines. Working for yourself in a home-based business usually gives you the freedom to shop or do other things, like go to the post office and the bank when you wish (for the most part).

In addition to this, when I get stressed with work and need a quick break, do you know what I do? I mow my lawn. This accomplishes two things: It gives my mind the clearing out that it needs, and by mowing my lawn during the week, it also frees up my Saturday afternoon.

9. No Stupid, Arbitrary Rules

When you own a home-based business, you can usually dress like you wish, decorate your office how you wish, come in when you wish, and leave when you wish. You can set a vacation time and not worry about it having to be approved, and (depending on your type of business) you can take off any day you want. You don't have to follow any inane rules. For example, through intelligent

scheduling and working a little harder some days, my business employs the three-day-weekend rule quite frequently.

10. No Boss

I saved this one for last because it's a big deal to me — the fact that the boss is the person looking back at you from the mirror is a huge plus.

I didn't have many good bosses — I had a few good ones earlier in my career (Al H. from Playtogs and Pete M. from Travelport immediately spring to mind), but I found as I rose in the corporate structure, the bosses got worse and worse. The rules got sillier, and the structure less flexible. Early in my career when I was a retail clerk, if I needed a day off, Al could just plug in another name-tag-wearing schlep with almost no noticeable drop-off.

However, as my skills improved and it was harder it to replace me (or so I told myself), the requests for days off and vacations were met with less enthusiasm. And I was expected to dress better, too. In addition, office politics started rearing its ugly head. Any idea I came up with was met with suspicion; who would take the credit was a big deal.

I have little patience for things like this. As far as work goes, I am interested in doing a good job, not in who gets credit for it. I dislike endless meetings and indecision, and am quite grating and difficult to deal with when I'm hit with red tape and office politics. So, being my own boss is a HUGE plus.

I suspect many people reading this book are a little like that. If you see yourself in any of the preceding examples, it's a good bet you will like working for yourself in a home-based business.

Chapter 9

COUNT ON THE UNEXPECTED HAPPENING

One of the best lessons I ever learned comes from doing home improvement projects. In short, the lesson is that the unexpected is always around the corner and can turn a seemingly simple project into a difficult one. Most people who are starting a business don't think of this. If they did, many of them would have second thoughts. I don't want to dampen your enthusiasm, but be prepared for many unexpected and time-consuming things to crop up when you start a business. As I said, it's a bit like doing home improvement projects.

Recently, my wife wanted a new light in the dining room. Never mind that my male brain thought the old one was fine; her female brain was horrified at the prospect of the old light hanging there even *one more day*, and she decided it had to be changed before our weekend visitors came. So anyway, I went to the attic to change the wiring for the new light, but unknown to me, the previous owner had wired the dimmer switch backwards (but it still worked).

This light had a dimmer on one wall, and a regular up-and-down switch on the other. However, I didn't really notice it was wired backwards. So I rewired it correctly (thus causing it to actually be *incorrect* in relation to the other switch), and when I thought I was done, I turned the power back on. Nothing. Well, nothing but a very troubling *huuum*. When working with electricity, that's *never* a good sound.

Result? Scratch one circuit breaker.

This project had already taken longer than I wanted, and now I had to go to the store to buy a new circuit breaker. Of course, having not bought circuit breakers in a few years, I forgot that I needed type A of a particular model. I bought type B. Type B didn't fit (although it looked like it should).

By now this was *really* taking longer than I wanted, so, even though it went against all logic, I tried to make it fit.

Ten minutes of persuasion with my rubber mallet yielded no results, so back to the store I went for another breaker. This time, I brought the old one with me (which I should have done in the first place), and bought type A.

Back home type A *still* wouldn't fit. Apparently my earlier persuasion with a mallet had bent the metal part the breaker slides into. A few taps with a hammer and a screwdriver, and success — it was now straight, and the breaker slid in.

Back to the attic. Then my wife told me, "Skip the dimmer switch — I don't like it anyway. Let's just use the one switch." I paused for a second, realizing that had she told me this three hours ago, I could have avoided all this. Anyway, I rewired it all correctly (I really am a pretty good electrician), and we now have a nice new light.

My point in telling this story is to illustrate the multitude of things that can go wrong with just about anything you do. If it's something you don't do often, budget *way* more time than you think you will need. This simple "half hour" job took me four hours.

Things That Seem Simple Often Aren't

Many aspects of your business will be harder than you think. And (as usual) many starting entrepreneurs are blind to this. Here's an example from my own experience.

In my first business, I created and sold direct-mail coupons. The idea was to have 30 local business coupons in the pack, and have the pack sent to 10,000 local households. This meant I had to get 10,000 of each coupon printed. The printer didn't collate the coupons, so I received 30 boxes, each containing 10,000 of a single coupon. I then paid a mailing service to sort them and stuff the envelopes. It worked out okay, but profits were very small.

For the second run, I decided to do the sorting and stuffing myself. I figured it would take a few nights to sort them.

That was my mistake. It took more than a few nights — it took a few *weeks* to do this. Think about it: 30 boxes, each with 10,000 coupons. My father and I devised a rack that held piles of all 30 coupons, like a post office mail rack. What you had to do was grab one from each slot in the rack (remember, there are 30), put the pile of 30 in an envelope, seal the envelope, and affix the mailing label. Taking into account refilling the rack and getting more envelopes ready, it took about a minute for each package.

So the entire job would take 10,000 minutes. That means it would take one person working nonstop for 24 hours, almost seven days. It would take four people, each working eight hours a day, almost five days.

Well, I didn't have four people willing to work eight hours a day. I *did* have a few friends who were willing to help in the evening. The trouble was, we were all in our early twenties, so I had to bribe them with beer (this is the law when you want friends to help you for free).

So I know for a fact that it takes four people almost four weeks of evenings to do the job. (Subtract a few days if you substitute coffee for beer, but then you're also subtracting the four people, so maybe that doesn't work.)

Why I didn't calculate this beforehand, I'll never know. I just figured, "Oh, this'll be easy." Well, it wasn't.

Not to mention how difficult it was to bring 10,000 bulk mail letters to the post office, which took me three trips in my little car. I could elaborate on other obstacles, but the whole experience is painful to remember.

Believe it or not, many people who are starting home-based businesses fail to think of obvious obstacles. Because if they did, many of them would have second thoughts. Thinking how much work something is tends to dampen enthusiasm.

I know someone who was going to start marketing a craft product he made out of a specific car part that "hot rod" drivers commonly replace. He was going to get this specific, hard-to-find part from Internet trading sites. In other words, the supply for his entire product line would be reliant on individual people selling unwanted parts. I asked, "How will you get the parts for 100 orders?" He didn't have a good answer to this question, so he quickly changed the subject — it was something that he really didn't want to think about.

I also know someone who wanted to start a painting service, but he did not have a truck or minivan or similar vehicle. So it was *very* difficult for him to transport ladders and five-gallon pails of paint to his various jobs. Transportation was something he really didn't think about at first. Suffice it to say, he got a van really soon.

Hey, I myself thought writing was easy until I got a complicated 20-page job. Ever write 20 pages on a boring subject? It's a lot of things, but "easy" isn't one of them.

In addition to underestimating the work involved, it's also very common to overestimate sales. Remember in my first business when I figured on 30 different coupons per package? That was because the printer would print them in a sheet of 30 — I got the best price that way. So my costs were fixed — whether I sold 30 or 25, the printer would still use an entire sheet, and my mail pack would still have to go to 10,000 households.

I thought selling 30 coupons would be easy. It wasn't. I ended up discounting a lot of them just to fill the pack, and I bartered a few away as well. My profit was slim indeed. I had overestimated my sales by a lot.

The lesson here is to always remember that nothing is as easy as it seems. Allot yourself the time and resources to make sure every angle is covered.

Chapter 10

NICHE MARKETS

I'll never forget the first time I knew, beyond any doubt, that I would eventually work for myself. I was 20 years old, and working in retail. Every day, I ate lunch by myself at the same pizza shop. Predictably, I got to know the owner, Jim, quite well.

So one day I walked in, and there was Jim behind the counter, reading a magazine. I ordered my usual, and Jim put down the magazine and started making my lunch. It was then that I saw the name of the magazine he was reading. It was called *Pizza World*.

Pizza World?

Yes, he was reading an actual magazine called *Pizza World*.

I asked Jim if I could see it, and he let me take a copy home. It was that night, when I read that issue of *Pizza World*, that my whole outlook on work and business changed. Here was a magazine I never saw on any newsstand — indeed, I had never heard of it. Yet it had a circulation of about 30,000. Inside, it was filled with articles and stories about running a pizza place, and more important, it was filled with advertisers, many of whom made their living selling products and services *exclusively* to little independent pizza places.

I was almost in shock as I realized that this was a little self-contained universe, right under my nose. There were pizza trade shows, there were pizza marketing newsletters, there were advertising agencies that *only* wrote ads for pizza places. There were even ads for custom pizza boxes (because, let's face it — it would be pretty silly for every pizza place in town to have the same "you've tried the rest, now try the best" slogan).

I was stunned that this magazine even existed, and I was stunned that people actually made a living selling things to pizza places.

I started to think. Almost every neighborhood or town has a pizza place — some have three or four. I then looked at my road atlas and was overwhelmed at how many towns there were just within 50 miles of me. Hundreds of little pizza places right in my area. Imagine how many there are in the country? Imagine if you had a product or service that could really be used by pizza places? And you could reach most of them with an ad in *Pizza World*? With very little competition? What if you could sell it to just one pizza place per county?

My mind raced.

Well, I'll admit I never came up with a pizza product. I never worked in a pizza place, so I didn't know much about the business. But that magazine taught me a valuable lesson: There are thousands of these little universes out there. All you have to do is open your eyes. *Opportunity is everywhere you look. It's just sort of "hiding."*

Just based on the above example, there's a separate universe for auto parts stores, car washes, framing stores, karate schools, daycare facilities, septic tank cleaning, painting, plumbing, etc. Every one of them is a little niche.

There are enough little universes and niches out there that almost *everyone* has a skill or an idea that can be useful in one of these little universes. And with tools like the Internet, there is no reason why someone — anyone — with a little bit of smarts and some guts can't make a good living working from home, offering something to the niche he or she knows a little bit about.

Working for yourself (or successfully running your business) begins with seeing an opportunity where most people do not. Most people would see a magazine called *Pizza World* and give it less pause than what's on TV tonight.

But not you. Not anymore. Hey, even if you already have a business, I'll bet you can think of a niche you can specialize in. It could be the start of something really big.

Think of all the things you've done in your life. The different jobs you've had. The different experiences you've had. I'll bet for each job you've had, there's something you know about that industry that the general public does not. Is there a service you can provide to that industry?

Perhaps you worked at a pizza place in your teens and early twenties, and maybe even became the night manager. You know all about pizza places — and about their customers. In fact, while you were working there, you probably said things like, "Man, the owner doesn't know what he's doing. If I ran this place, I'd …"

And, now as an adult, you've traded in your pizza apron for a college degree and a job in marketing. So you know pizza places, and you know marketing. Hmmm … maybe you can place an ad in *Pizza World* offering to assist pizza places with their marketing and advertising. Remember, all you need is a few clients — imagine if just two or three per state paid you $500 per year for your monthly "pizza place only" marketing newsletter and creative ads. (To make it desirable, tell them that you only allow one per county to sign up.)

Some pizza place owners will tell you to take a hike. In fact, most will. But there are a few who, if your newsletter is good enough, would happily pay, even if just to keep their competition shut out.

The beauty of something like this (which happens in more industries than you think) is that you write 12 newsletters and 12 packs of monthly ads. You can play golf the rest of the month if you want to (you won't — you'll be trying to get into other niches — but you *could*).

You need to find these niche market nuggets and mine them. How do you find them? OPEN YOUR EYES and notice things like odd little magazines called *Pizza World*.

Tip: Go to a big bookstore such as Barnes & Noble or Borders and look at their magazines. You will find all sorts of "odd" magazines. Buy a few and look at the ads. That should give you plenty of inspiration.

Other Types of Niches

I'm a big fan of horror, and while looking on the Internet for scary stuff for my basement, I came across the website of an artist who specializes in spooky paintings. Here's a guy who's an artist who has carved himself a niche selling his prints to the world. I bought several. I buy many products from small, home-based entrepreneurs: owl figurines (I

like owls, too); sea otter shirts for my wife; old, out-of-print books.

Back when I was making custom golf clubs, I began by selling them on eBay. This is a great way to test the market for a product. (There are entire books about the inner workings of eBay, so I won't go into detail here. Suffice it to say, listing a product is surprisingly easy: go online, sign up, and follow the instructions.)

My eBay experience let me know there was a market for my product, so I built a website. I eventually shut the business down, but the fact is, I found a little niche (custom golf clubs) and comfortably fit a product into it.

Niche markets are everywhere. It's up to you to fit yourself into one (or create one). Perhaps you have a talent that is perfect for a niche, or you can make a product, or you have some professional knowledge or skill that a niche could find useful. It's a big world out there — find your niche and carve your place.

A Small Numbers Game

A few years ago I wrote the following on an online business forum. It puts starting a home-based business into perspective:

> … here's one of the key things that keeps me going in my entrepreneurial endeavors: It's a HUGE world out there with an untold number of different flavors, varieties, tastes, wants, and needs. Knowing that, I've always felt that there HAS to be something I can offer or do that will result in just 30 people or companies paying me two to three thousand dollars each per year.

I wasn't looking to make a million bucks or break through with a best-selling product. I didn't want to be Wal-Mart, or even Dan-Mart. All I wanted was 30 companies or people in the entire world to pay me two to three thousand dollars a year for my services. That's $60,000 to $90,000 per year. Heck, if I looked hard enough, I could probably find 30 *local* companies to pay me two grand annually just to clean their offices or something.

When you look at it in numbers like that, all of a sudden succeeding in a home-based business doesn't seem so daunting, does it?

Chapter 11

GET OUT OF YOUR COMFORT ZONE

In order to succeed, you will have to expand your worldview and get out of your comfort zone. What I mean by that is you have to realize not everyone thinks like you think; not everyone wants what you want; and not everyone does things like you do.

In fact, let's take this a step further — not everyone thinks like you *and even like the people you know*. It's a big country out there, and an even bigger world.

I realize this sounds like an obvious point, but it's really not — remember the New Business Blinders. Sure, we acknowledge the diversity in different tastes when we go clothes shopping, but this acceptance of diversity hits a wall when it comes to business ideas. Why, I don't know, but it does.

To give you an example, when I told a friend of mine about my writing business, he rolled his eyes. "Who would pay someone to write?" he said. He simply could not *imagine* a person or a business actually *paying* for a writer. Do you know why he thought this? Because nobody he knows ever needed to hire a writer. So, in his very limited worldview (and his exact words), "*Nobody* would ever need to hire a writer."

That's like saying nobody would ever wear a medium-sized shirt. Aren't we *all* XXL? Of course we're not.

This isn't to say that every single idea you can think of will have a market, but if you have any kind of gut feeling that your business idea is a good one, it probably does have a market, despite what your family and friends may think.

From my *Pizza World* revelation (and my experience doing business with freelance computer programming), I *knew* that there were people and companies out there that needed my writing skills. And I was right.

Here's something interesting: I advertise on Google by paying for certain key words and phrases. When someone searches for those phrases, my ad appears. If someone clicks on my ad, which brings them to my website, I pay a certain amount (like 50 cents). Here are some of the results of my ads for one day, November 19, 2006. (These numbers are for the US only.)

Key word/phrase	Impressions	Clicks
business writer	244	8
letter writer	171	3
professional writer	76	3
writing for business	4	2

Now let's look at what this means. This means that on this particular day, 244 people searched Google for a "business writer." Over two hundred! In one day. That sort of puts to shame my friend's assumption that *nobody* would need to hire a writer.

Now, out of those 244 people, eight clicked on my ad. Out of those eight, one or two likely contacted me. This may not be a big deal, until you realize that these few people are *very* interested in my service. After all, they searched for what I do, clicked on my ad, and then contacted me.

Many times, when someone hires me, it leads to thousands of dollars in billed services.

Are you beginning to see the obvious futility in having a narrow worldview?

> **There is a market for almost any reasonable service or business you can think of.**

Heck, let's go *way* out on a limb and say that even if you had a service where people paid you to beat them up, you could make a living.

Are you laughing yet? You won't be in a second …

Just call yourself a dominatrix.

The joke is on the people who think "whatever" can't work. Plenty of odd business ideas can work. Success or failure almost always resides in the execution and the marketing of the idea. (No, this doesn't mean the party website idea mentioned earlier has merit.)

Take Some Advice — or Not

Understand that it is natural for people who are not entrepreneurs to be down on almost *any* business idea. They'll say things like my friend did: "Who would *ever* need that?"

> **Here's a tip that has always served me well in my life: Do not take advice from people who are not doing better than you are.**

This tip means you should not take financial advice from people who are not rich; you should not take relationship advice from people who are not in happy, successful relationships; and you should not take business advice from people who are not in business.

By and large, this means *not* listening to advice from your family and friends who don't own businesses. They have very little to offer you in terms of business advice unless they truly understand business. I warn you here because everybody, and I mean *everybody*, will have an opinion on your new venture. Most of the opinions won't be favorable, either. So unless you really feel the people offering the advice know what they are talking about, ignore them. For example, your uncle who drives a cement truck for the county likely knows very little about running an advertising or computer repair business.

Family is great to turn to for support when one is ill, and they are second to none for those times when you feel you need a little *extra* stress and turmoil in your life. Go seek them out for that (and if you *really* want stress, invite several of the not-speaking-to-each-other members to the same party). But you can generally ignore their words of wisdom when it comes to business advice. Naturally there are exceptions: If Uncle Elmo works for an insurance firm, he may have some advice on what type of insurance you may need for your business.

Now, when I say "family," I mean your mom, dad, sisters, brothers, uncles, cousins, second cousins, and even that guy who's not really an uncle but for some reason you call uncle. I do *not* mean your spouse, who is vital to your success. Your spouse is a partner in your business, whether his or her name is on it or not, so he or she has every right to be critical, to offer input, to open the books, to help with advertising and marketing, etc. Only the foolish business-person ignores spousal concerns. If you pick anyone to listen to, listen to your spouse.

Chapter 12

SOME THINGS ARE SIMPLY WORTH PAYING FOR

I'm putting this topic in the Mind section because it's a mindset more than anything else — and that mindset is getting over the "cheapness" hump and paying people to do work or provide services for you.

Listen — some things are simply worth paying for. And this is coming from a guy who's pretty big on do-it-yourself. In the past, I prepared a lot of my own business marketing materials — like my website. I thought it was good enough, but I was really just fooling myself. I know now that my DIY mentality cost me business. Period.

That's because the basic problem with DIY can be boiled down to a simple phrase: *Homemade stuff looks homemade.*

And obviously *homemade* marketing materials do not encourage people to do business with you.

Business cards and brochures made on an inkjet printer scream, "We have no money." A website built using a free online site builder says, "We do not care about presentation — oh, and we have no money either." Poor writing on any of your communication shouts out, "We simply don't care."

If you want to be taken seriously as a professional, you need to look and act the part. And part of looking and acting the part is to have professional-looking business materials. This means paying for them. And here's the kicker — we're really not looking at a whole lot of money.

Think about the message that home-made business cards convey: "I'm just starting out and not confident enough in my business to spend the $100 real cards would have cost me." That's what message you're giving out.

Because that's really what it boils down to: the person with the homemade card does not truly think the business will work. Otherwise, nice business cards would be one of the first things purchased. They aren't *that* expensive.

Well, if someone is not confident enough to whip out their credit card and risk a hundred bucks on business cards, then I'm not confident enough to do business with them. (More on business cards in Chapter 28).

This homemade attitude happens a lot on websites, too. I can't count the number of websites out there that just look terrible. They have a boring Times New Roman font (which is the default on most programs), and the same stale pictures that every clip art program has been trotting out for years. These websites were either made with free online site-building services or by using cheap software bought at an office supply store.

These cheap programs are great for personal websites where people put up pictures of their pets and write fairly bad poetry, but they are ill-suited for business.

The sheer number of awful, cheap websites out there is proof that people just don't care. But I'll tell you this: Nobody does business with a cheap-looking website. I'd be doing you a disservice if I told you anything different.

I know this from experience: I built my own websites for years. I had my first website in 1995, and I can (sloppily) code HTML.

So, essentially what I'm saying is I know enough to be dangerous. And I thought I could get by with my own homemade website.

And you know what — I could. To a point. My homemade websites looked like a professional website circa 1998 — but we were into the new millennium. Since Internet years are like dog years, my 1998 web design skills were akin to a Model T mechanic working on a fuel-injected engine. My site just looked shabby and old. So I found a good web designer and paid to have a professional website built.

Now, even though I paid a professional, my website skills still served me well. Since I understood HTML and a website's structure, I really only needed *one* page designed, and I took it from there by copying and pasting. But let me tell you, I noticed a *big* difference as soon as my new website went live. In a word, I was truly seen as a professional.

Here are several skills it is well worth paying for:

- Design of business cards, brochures, and other printed advertising material

- Website design

- Copywriting for point-of-sale materials such as brochures, websites, proposals, and sales letters (unless you are a skilled writer)

- Accounting/tax preparation services

- Legal services

I'm not saying that if you have any real skill in these areas you should not do things on your own. Just remember: Homemade stuff looks homemade.

Chapter 13

HOW HARD CAN IT BE?

This chapter title may seem odd coming after the chapter where I tell you to hire professionals for many things. However, stay with me, because it's really more about a mindset than actually doing everything yourself.

One of the best questions you can ask yourself is, "How hard can it possibly be?" I urge you to start asking yourself this question all the time. It opens a lot of doors. Because often the answer is, "Not all that hard."

For example, take building a basic website.

Can you build a basic website? Most of you will say no, thinking it's something that is *way* beyond you. But building a basic website is really *very* easy. If you can write a letter, you can build a basic website. I never would have known this if I had not asked myself, "How hard can it possibly be?" I would have been like 99.9 percent of the population who think building a website is something they can't do.

My basic message is that things that seem *way* beyond you really aren't if you just ask, "Well, how hard can it possibly be?"

From asking this question, I learned the following skills:

- How to maintain my own website

- How to be proficient at using many computer applications

- How to make my own golf clubs

- How to do almost all my own electrical, carpentry, and plumbing work

None of these tasks is very hard. The biggest roadblocks are fear, uncertainty, and an unwillingness to devote the time to learning something new. Also, as humans, we tend to assume we can't do things.

If you knew how easy it is to make a golf club from parts, you'd be stunned. If you can use glue and a hacksaw, and follow very simple instructions, you can *easily* make a golf club. But most people would not even try.

Or, if a pipe in your home bursts, most people panic and run in circles, getting wet until the plumber arrives. I was one of those people until, while waiting, I asked myself the magic question.

I found out that replacing the damaged pipe was pretty simple indeed. It took a practice run or two, and yes, it involved using an acetylene torch. And truth be told, it wasn't that difficult.

There is no huge trick to basic plumbing, basic electrical work, building a basic website, or most other seemingly hard tasks. I'm not saying it's easy to be a professional electrician, a professional golf club maker, or a professional web designer. It isn't. But I *am* saying that the basics are within reach of just about everyone.

This mindset is important in a home-based business, because you are going to have to learn some seemingly unpleasant and out-of-reach things. For example, if you operate a home-based business, you should learn how to take credit card payments. Taking payment by credit cards will not only make your life easier, it will make your customers' lives easier, and it will increase your business. Don't say, "I can't" or "I don't understand it." People who succeed don't say things like that. Instead, they look at something challenging and say, Well, how hard can it be?

Fear and uncertainty disappear when you ask that simple question.

Chapter 14

STOP DREAMING AND START DOING

If you are going to own your own business, it is essential, *absolutely essential*, that you actually *do* the things you KNOW you are supposed to do, and you KEEP doing them.

It sounds simple, but it isn't. There are volumes of motivational books on the subject and plenty of life coaches who have made multimillion-dollar careers out of simply telling people to get off their butts and *do* something.

Most people are *great* talkers. But very few actually follow through.

Think about this for a second. How hard do you work at your current job? For most people, the true answer is probably "not very hard."

I've been around hundreds of corporate people, salespeople, construction workers, laborers, delivery people, doctors, lawyers, accountants, auto mechanics … you name it. If I had to guess, I'd say most people actually work about half to two-thirds of the time they are paid for. The rest of the time is spent daydreaming, chatting with coworkers, thinking about personal problems, getting a drink, going to the bathroom, surfing the web, taking up a collection for Bonnie who is away with gallstone problems (so she claims), or a million other time-wasting activities.

Oh, we all have our busy times, but even fast-food workers get to slack off after the lunch rush.

My point is that this time wasting *must stop* when you own your own business. Oh, you can still have idle time, but you can only do so *after* you do your work. When you own your own business, nobody tells you what to do. This is a good thing for some, but it's not so good for many people. As much as we like to say we're self-starters, most of us would be clueless without the boss (or the company) somehow making the work appear.

I have a friend — let's call him Kyle — who always had these great ideas for businesses. He had a new scheme or idea almost weekly. Kyle was always telling me how he was going to do this, or buy this software and learn how to do that, or offer a service to put people's pictures on a mug, or … whatever. All of these grand plans. Do you know how many times Kyle actually went to a county building to officially start a business?

Zero.

Once, he bought some software for designing websites, and he wanted me and two other guys to all chip in. We'd all learn this software together and become a web design firm. I passed, because I knew Kyle's way of doing things. Do you know how many hours he actually booted up the software and delved into it? Maybe three. Then the ball game came on, someone brought beer over, and the plans became a distant memory.

He *knew* that if he just learned how to use the software, he'd at least have a shot at becoming a web designer, but he didn't do it.

Many times, the difference between someone who is successful and someone who isn't is that the successful person simply does the things that need to be done.

Let's look at an example. When I was in high school, I wasn't very popular with girls. It wasn't because I didn't want to be: in my imagination, I was the object of desire of roughly 75 percent of the female population of Minisink Valley High, who routinely fought over me in a decidedly clothes-ripping manner. These battles usually took place in a cooling rain on a hot summer's day, and the winner would always ask me to help her with her wet clothes. Hey, if you're going to dream, dream big.

Anyway, my point is, I really wanted some female companionship. However, instead of actually asking someone out, I'd park myself within 20 feet or so of the object of my desire and — get ready for this — *hope and wish really hard.*

Suffice it to say, my approach didn't work. In fact, the hope-and-wish method is probably one of the least effective courtship techniques available to men.

Do you know who got the girls instead? *The guys who actually asked them out.*

I learned real quick, and after high school, I started adopting the ask-them-out method. My female companionship rate rose quite a bit (which has its own set of problems, but that's for another book). The same principle applies in business. *You have to start the business, and you actually have to do the work.* If you don't, all you have are hope and wishes, which are pretty meaningless.

The Walking Test

I'm going to try to save some of you a lot of money and heartache in your plans to own a home-based business. Here's a test to show you if you have what it takes to be a business owner. I want you to try this very simple exercise: I want you to start walking.

Rain or shine, hot or cold, you go out (or go to the gym, or use a treadmill) and walk a mile every day. It can be in the morning or the evening — whatever fits your schedule. But, barring *real* illness or a huge blizzard, you can't miss a day.

If, after a month, you are still walking, you have what it takes to at least give yourself a fighting chance at making it on your own. If you dropped out, thought the exercise was stupid, or whatever, you can certainly still go into business, but I'm not sure I'd recommend it. If you gave up on or couldn't finish a simple walking exercise, how can you expect to succeed in business, which is a *lot* harder than walking? If you didn't finish the month, it's my guess that your business will most likely fail. (You could still fail even if you passed the walking test, but at least you'll go down fighting.)

The point behind this exercise is that everyone is a great starter, but very few people actually do the things they need to do on a regular, consistent basis. I'm sure you're thinking, "Oh, I can walk for a month … I don't need to do this."

Yes, you do. Know why? Because I'll bet most of you can't do it.

I'll bet that one day, something will come up and you'll think, "Ahh … I'll walk two miles tomorrow." Well, I have to say, customers won't buy that excuse.

So do the exercise (pardon the pun). You'll be happy you did.

To-Do Lists

I'm a big fan of to-do lists. They keep me on track with the things I need to do, and they ensure nothing gets lost. I use three methods:

1. **My yellow legal pad**

    My yellow legal pad's to-do list is written weekly. Most items are jobs I have to do that week, and I cross them off as I do them. Sometimes items get carried over. A one-week list works for me, but you may be comfortable with daily or monthly lists. Just be consistent.

2. **My desk calendar**

    I have an at-a-glance 8½" x 11" desk calendar. It opens like a book and has each month on a single page, plus a page for each day. I only use the whole-month view. This allows me to write something in for a day that's months from now, and it ensures I won't forget it when the month comes.

3. **My white board**

    I have a dry-erase white board hanging near my desk with columns for several key items: immediate projects that I'm working on, next week's projects, who needs to be invoiced (I invoice every two weeks), and unpaid invoices I have out.

I highly suggest the white board. It shows your entire business at a glance.

Change How You Spend Your Time

Another key difference between successful home-based business owners and everyone else isn't natural talent, or smarts, or even hard work — it's how they spend their time.

Let's return to the example I gave earlier about learning how to take credit card payments. When I mention this to people wanting to start a business I'm often asked, "Well, how do I learn how to do that?" My answer is very simple: "Go online, search for credit card merchants, and read how it's done. It's going to take a little effort, and it's going to take some time."

You know what most people say in reply?

They say "oh" in a rather dejected tone.

Digging deeper usually yields something like, "I don't have time to do that." What they really mean is, "I don't have other things I'm willing to give up."

A busy life filled with TV, social activities, going out, and the constant company of friends is going to impede your business success, especially when you're starting out. There's no way around this.

I can use myself as an example — I hardly know any characters on TV programs. I just don't have time to get wrapped up in TV and watch any shows on a regular basis. It's not that I don't watch TV — football Sunday is still sacred to me, the Yankees are on in the background if they are playing, and I'll catch an occasional show that might interest me. I also love movies, and have an extensive collection. I don't want to sound like one of those annoying "I don't own a TV" people (have you ever noticed people like that always seem to make it a point to mention that they don't own a TV?).

So I watch TV when I can/have time — but not on any kind of regular basis. I don't do *anything* on a regular basis, really — I don't have an activity that takes a night or two every week (like clubs, bowling, or such). There's little room in my life for that — running a successful business almost becomes your hobby. Everything else is secondary and needs to work around that. It's not that I don't take time off — I take plenty of time off. But I don't have a life full of activities that I need to schedule work around.

As for my social life, I have excellent friends, but my friends are not a constant part of my day-to-day life (or even week-to-week life) — I simply do not have the time for that. I don't socialize much — most of my socializing is with my wife. And many of my friends are people I see two or three times a year (and we're fine with that).

In knowing many successful business owners, they all seem to be the same way — the social calendar is a mix of mostly family and a very occasional evening spent with friends. There is very little "hanging out" with the old gang.

This is especially difficult for some people — someone who goes out golfing every Sunday, bowling every Tuesday, and watches two TV programs religiously every week is going to have a hard time keeping that up and still running a successful home-based business. I know I couldn't do it. In essence, you are going to have to choose between your business and your bowling buddies. And I'll be the first to admit — it's a hard choice.

Again, I don't want to sound like owning a business is all work and no play — I take plenty of time off, and I play whenever I get the chance. And now that the business is running nicely, I probably *could* take on a bowling night or weekly golf game.

But when you're starting out, having a scheduled life where things like weekly TV programs, constant web surfing and Internet chatting, or social activities and/or constant visits with friends are probably going to impede your success.

In my failed businesses, I kept my social calendar just as it was (which included weekly bowling, a weekly gaming night with friends, parties all the time, and plenty of nights in the bar). It's little wonder I had no time to really *learn* anything about business. I was too busy. I've since changed the way I go about things, and changed how full my life is. The effect on my business has been profound. I even found time to write this book.

Once your business is rolling and you are making a real living, *that's* the time you can perhaps start easing social activities back into your life. But when you are starting out, running a successful business almost always requires a change in your priorities and how you spend your time.

Chapter 15

YOU DO REALIZE YOU'RE THE ONE WHO MAKES THE WORK APPEAR, RIGHT?

There's a great episode of the TV show *Seinfeld* where George gets a new, somewhat undefined office job (easily the best kind). On his first day, he's handed the "Penske file" to work on. Of course, George doesn't do any work on this prized account, but that's not my point. My point is, he went to a job, and as if by magic, the work showed up and was handed to him. All he had to do was walk in the door and there was something meaningful for him to do.

If you stop for a minute to think about it, that defines just about any job you can have. Someone (a company) needs a certain type of task done, and they exchange assets (salary, benefits) with individual people to work on these tasks. Even in a somewhat entrepreneurial job such as selling cars, there

is still a certain amount of hand-holding. The dealership provides the inventory, a desk, and a steady flow of customers walking through the door. The salesperson simply needs to close the deal.

But in your own business, you are totally on your own. Nobody "gives" you work — you have to somehow create it. Sure, the basic structure is the same (someone pays you to do something or provide a service), but the *automatic* part of it is no more. You can't just show up and expect to be provided for. It all comes from you.

This is a pretty sobering thought for most people.

You almost have to create a market for whatever it is you do. Oh, sure, there is plenty of need for certain services. A good carpenter will almost never go hungry. But what about someone who makes jewelry and wants to sell it online? How are they going to find the market for their product? Jewelry trade shows? Craft magazines? Online advertising? All three?

No matter what your home-based business is, this is a question that needs a clear answer — you are going to have to think about how the work will appear. Because it won't just show up. You have to provide it all.

Making the work appear is one of the hardest parts of owning a home-based business. It's something you are going to have to really think about. You have to have a good idea of how and why the work will show up. I can't tell you how to go about doing that. For every business, the answer will be different. However, there are three basic points that are true for all businesses looking for customers/work:

1. Define who needs your product or service

2. Figure out how to reach them

3. Reach them with an appealing message (there's plenty on advertising and marketing in this book to help you)

If you do all three, the chances are the work will begin to appear. But you have to do them. In other words, there is no hoping or wishing — your efforts, and your efforts alone, are going to make the work appear. You cannot just start the business and hope for the best — it doesn't work that way.

The New Business Blinders I occasionally talk about are in full force here. People get all excited about *what* they will do and don't think about *who* will need them to do it.

Lose the "Job Mentality"

Most of us have a job mentality, and it's important that you lose that.

To better explain this, I'll tell a brief story. I was once watching TV with a friend, and on the particular show we were watching was one of those rugged, individualistic photographers. He was jet-setting to exotic locales, snapping pictures wherever he went, being chased by cannibals because he stole the sacred coconut ... So my friend says, "Gee, I would like to be a photographer."

To begin, I could think of several reasons why he *shouldn't* be a photographer, most glaring of which was the fact that he took lousy photographs. Really, taking shots of backyard fall foliage with your $129 digital camera does not make you a great photographer, even if your camera has a zoom button and you use the "artsy" black-and-white setting. My friend was also decidedly out of shape, and could never run from cannibals. Granted, he would probably make a nice stew once he was caught, but that's a really poor (and short-lived) career choice.

But, in addition to his lack of skill and athletic ability, my friend gave another clue that he would never make it as a globe-trotting photographer. His next statement after "Gee, I would like to be a photographer," was, "I wonder how you get a job like that?"

Well, *National Geographic* and your local newspaper notwithstanding, most photographers don't really have "jobs." They are freelancers, either selling their shots to magazines, tabloids, and newspapers; or they set up shop locally and do weddings and other local professional photo shoots.

Usually, a profession like this is started out of love for the craft — someone loves taking pictures so much that they develop a real skill for it (and it is a real skill — anyone can take a snapshot, but a professional takes a photograph). They then develop so much skill that others begin to take notice, and soon they are doing a friend's wedding. Or they send some interesting photos to many magazines, and finally one magazine buys one.

In other words, there are very few "photographer" openings in the local Help Wanted section of the newspaper. If you want to be a photographer, you, for the most part, have to lose the job mentality and not think, "How can I get a job like that?"

It's the same thing for business. If you want to own a business — any business — you have to think way beyond "job." For my own business, I didn't worry about "how do I get a job as a writer?" I simply put my writing out there in the form of a website, and advertised. Yes, people "hire" me, but they don't hire me in the classic sense — they hire me for a specific project, and when it's over, I stop working for them. Until they need another writing project.

But it's me, putting my skill out there that makes the work appear. It doesn't appear because I arbitrarily show up at an office.

Chapter 16

DON'T IGNORE THE THINGS YOU DON'T UNDERSTAND

A contractor I know used to say, "Word of mouth is the best advertising." I'd have taken him at his word, except I know for a fact that he hadn't tried *any* advertising except one tiny Yellow Pages ad, once. How he arrived at that conclusion, I'll never know. What he's really saying is, "I don't really understand advertising and I don't want to think about it." Instead of admitting this, the subject is swept under the rug and ignored. This would be fine if my friend was busy all the time, but he isn't. He could certainly stand to explore advertising a little bit. I've tried to discuss it with him, but the topic is not even allowed on the table. He doesn't understand it, so that's that.

There's nothing unusual about his response. Most adults tend to shy away from things that they don't understand. When we're kids, we love to explore and discover new things. We want to see what's inside a Super Ball, how deep that hole is, or what happens when we combine six different chemicals in a large Coke bottle, sit a GI Joe on top of it, and throw a match through a little hole on the bottle.

As children, we're filled with wonder. As we age, we become more and more close-minded and resistant to things that we don't understand. This is not helpful to someone in a home-based business because you are going to have to learn about a lot of new things.

In my first business, well before the Internet was a viable resource, I wanted to accept payment by credit card. A little research got me the needed information, but to be honest, it was more than I wanted to read. Forms and percentages and more forms and phone lines and terminals and merchant accounts. Do you know what I did with it? I threw all that information out — out of sight, out of mind. And since I was now on mailing lists, I received more information — and I threw that out too. It was just too complicated, and I wanted no part of it. I completely shut it off.

Too bad, because my very first prospect asked me if we took credit cards. I'll bet I could have increased sales by a lot had I just sat down for an evening and figured out how to do it. Millions of places take credit cards: How hard could it really be?

But for some reason, I can't explain it … I didn't want to be bothered. It was just too hard, and I threw the information away.

If you find yourself doing something like this, stop. Immediately. Find some time and dive into whatever it is that you're having trouble understanding. Ask for help if you must.

Don't shy away from learning something new. It's one of the worst things you can do.

Here are a few examples of things that people seem to have trouble with, and where you can go to for help:

- *Advertising.* Call your local Yellow Pages company (or newspaper or direct-mail company) and ask for a salesperson. They will be more than happy to help you.

- *Credit cards.* Search online for "merchant accounts" or "accepting credit cards." PayPal is also a wonderful free resource that can really help you.

- *Websites.* Look online for a good web designer. If you can't afford that, your local community college is a good place to find students looking to build their portfolios who would love to build you a fairly serviceable website for a great price. Get in touch with faculty members; they are often happy to refer one or two of their best students. Just don't expect a professional web design job at a college student price. If you have the funds, I heartily recommend finding a pro. However, if your funds are limited, it's better to hire a college student learning web design than to not have a website at all.

- *Computers/email/Internet.* Again, paying a college student to tutor you on computers/email/Internet is a great investment. Trust me: Ask around at your local college; you will find plenty of eager takers.

Chapter 17

STOP WASTING TIME ON NONSENSE

Beginning home-based entrepreneurs can waste their time on a staggering amount of nonsense — all in the name of avoiding the real work.

Doing the actual *work* that makes money is hard. And scary. So thinking "I can't *really* start until my logo is perfect" is comforting and safe. And it can take days. Or weeks.

In my first business, the real work started when I made that first sales call. Everything up to that was preliminary busywork. Now, I admit that much of it was required — getting the business started, getting cards printed (with a basic logo), getting samples made, etc. These all had to be done before I could do the *real* work. But

they were small, inconsequential things that I rushed through. I wanted to go make money. Now.

An older and wiser person, I am somewhat impressed at my younger self in this regard — even at a young age, I recognized that in the beginning stages of a small home-based business, *everything* was secondary to making money. Of course, my youthful self squandered this exceptional insight, but my point is, there was very little time between the "let's start a business" conversation and the actual first day of sales calls. And that's the way it should be.

I mention this because it is very easy to get caught up in … nonsense. Things like researching on the Internet ad nauseam, or asking other people's opinions, or talking about business/making endless plans/waiting for just the right time to begin.

> **In a beginning home-based business, nothing is more important than producing income. *Nothing.* Everything else takes a back seat.**

Yes, there are preliminary tasks to get done, and depending on your business you may have to deal with zoning, insurance, etc., but if you aren't attempting to make money fairly quickly, your business will probably go nowhere. I say this from my own experience and from watching other businesses.

My own experience with nonsense came soon after I started my first business. As I stated earlier, I hated sales calls with a passion. So, after a while, I did what I could to avoid them. I started finding all kinds of things I could do that *seemed* like work, but really weren't. Things like attending the Chamber of Commerce trade show for all three days, telling myself I'd make valuable contacts. Instead, I talked to a few people I already knew and walked around, dropping my business card in all the "win a free service" fishbowls that were at most of the tables. (For the record, I won a free chimney sweep, which would have been wonderful if I had a chimney.)

I also spent a lot of time at bars. Again, I did this to "make business contacts," which, I'm sorry to say, does not include the cocktail waitress, no matter what I tried to tell myself. It was pretty sad, really — I sat there like I was some business big shot, and accumulated astronomical credit card debt,

while I was making absolutely no income. I went from go-getter to subconsciously living a fairly big lie in a pretty short time. All because I hated sales calls and did whatever I could to avoid making them.

I also wasted a lot of time on motivational books and tapes, writing down my goals, etc. In particular, I thought that writing down my goals would give me a real edge — as if having goals were profound. All the motivational material essentially said the same thing: Do the things you need to do. But that didn't keep me from eating this stuff up. And truth be told, I wasn't going anywhere, no matter what my "goal planner" said. I recently found an old notebook and laughed that I actually had had the gall to write that we'd have company cars in a year. This is before I had even cracked $1,000 in sales — who was I kidding?

So my purpose here is essentially to tell you that almost anything besides making money (or leading to making money) is probably a waste of time. I'm saying "almost" because of course there will be a few things you'll need to do that don't directly relate to sales/income. But I *am* saying that *excessive* time spent planning/going over lists/designing logos/endlessly researching/prospecting at the bar/listening to motivational tapes … all this is time probably better spent actually making money.

Don't kid yourself. You know if what you are doing is actually productive or if it's to avoid the real income-producing work. Make sure that your home-based business efforts are largely going to *actually producing* income, not *planning* how you're going to produce it.

Chapter 18

BEING NEAT MEANS BUSINESS

Years ago, a friend of mine had been asked to give a presentation on sales to a local contractor/builder association meeting. He brought me along as a copresenter, so I got to say a few words to the roomful of local tradesmen.

One of the things I suggested was that when making a sales call to bid on a job, they perhaps dress a little nicer than their standard work wear. I wasn't suggesting suits and ties, but I implied that maybe coming to bid on a remodeling job directly after a steamy hot day on the roof wasn't a good idea. Nothing kills a mood quite like a sweaty guy smelling of roof tar.

Well, I wasn't very well received. This was one rowdy bunch.

In fact, by the reaction I got, you'd have thought I outlawed beef jerky or something. Holy @#$%, was this group resistant to the idea. Catcalls and shouts of, "Well, what do you want us to do, keep more clothes in the truck?" and, "Nobody is impressed if we look neat" were randomly tossed out as I spoke. I tried to explain that it wasn't about trying to impress anyone, but instead merely trying to *avoid* a bad impression.

Well, they weren't having any of it. Except for one guy. One guy spoke up and agreed with me. He said he made it a point of going home and showering before going out on evening bids/sales calls.

He also happened to be the most successful contractor in the room. By a lot. Big surprise there …

We spoke privately after the presentation, and I asked him to expand on what he mentioned. He told me that he recognized the value of being neat, or more importantly, of *not* being sloppy. He wanted to portray an image of competence, and it started with himself. He figured that if *he* looked sloppy, one might assume his work would be sloppy. So it's not that he made it a point to look good — he made it a point to *not* look sloppy.

He hit the nail right on the head. He recognized that being neat probably didn't get him any *extra* business, but it probably prevented him from *losing* business. And that's really what it boils down to. With most home-based businesses, your dress and overall appearance won't gain you business, but they can certainly lose you business.

The same goes for your vehicle, your office, your place of business — they all reflect on your abilities. A sloppy vehicle means you are a sloppy person, and likely do sloppy work. A sloppy office is not a place clients want to visit — trust me on this.

A neat office has other benefits too. I have every piece of information I would ever need within easy reach. I know exactly where everything is at all times. I am very neat and particular about my work space, and more than once a client has been impressed at how fast I can come up with something. Because I am so orderly in my files, my desk, and my to-do lists, I simply don't lose things. (My wife may disagree on some of my neatness claims, but she isn't writing this book, is she?)

And I have to be honest — it helps in my business. I know where everything is, I keep good records and schedules, I am on time, etc. I don't know how to turn anyone else into a neat person, but if you want to succeed in your home-based business, make neatness a priority.

Dress for Success — or Not

I'd like to return to clothes for a minute, because there is one aspect I skipped.

I read a lot of business books, and most of them advocate dressing nicely even if you aren't seeing customers. They say things like, "If you look professional, you'll work better," or, "if you dress the part, you'll *feel* more like a professional."

I have to say, now that I work at home, I disagree with these claims. If I'm not seeing customers or I'm in my home office, I'll dress as I wish. Shaving is optional, too. I just don't need the motivational trick of dressing like a businessperson. Maybe some people do, and that's fine. But personally, I don't.

To me, one of the big perks of a home-based business is choice of clothing. For the most part, I can wear what is most comfortable. This means shorts and a T-shirt in the summer, and sweats and flannel shirts in the winter. And comfy slippers year round!

When I'm on the phone with big-time clients talking about the copy for their annual report, I'm in my sweats and NY Jets sweatshirt. If they could see me in person, I'd probably lose the account. I love this aspect of a home-based business, and am not about to give it up.

So, my advice to you in this regard is to always look good for clients, but wear what you feel comfortable in otherwise. If you feel more comfortable in business attire, even if you're working alone, so be it. Go right ahead and suit up. If you'd rather join me in wearing sweats, go for it. I also heartily recommend the brand "Old Friends" for slippers, especially during cold bouts of weather.

Chapter 19

DO THINGS THE RIGHT WAY, OR DON'T DO THEM

I want you to think about all of the jobs you ever had, and all the people you have ever worked with. How many people actually did things the right way, all the time? How many people took such care in their work that no shortcuts were taken, and everything was always done the way it was supposed to be done? Think about your experiences as a consumer of services: How many people out there actually perform their jobs the right way? How satisfied are you with the service you receive?

The sad truth is, someone doing a good job happens so infrequently and is so extraordinary, that it's almost a pleasant surprise when it actually happens. Yet I'm sure, everyone thinks they always do good work.

I'd say most people's work is barely passable. Most people do the bare minimum to keep their jobs, and little more. You'll hear phrases like "they don't pay me enough for that" or "good enough" or "why should I work hard if Emily doesn't?" … As if modeling your professional career after Emily in accounting, who once ate four plates of hot wings on a dare and dated that greasy guy who smelled like Brylcreem, is a smart move.

By and large, we've become a society where "good enough" is the gold standard with regard to work.

You can't do that in your home-based business.

You have to be *on* nearly all the time, and you have to give your absolute best on every single job. There is no slacking off, no "good enough," no "well, I'm not getting paid enough for this." Everything you do reflects on you, and the customer is dealing with you, not a nameless employee in a big company.

In almost every job you ever had, you were somewhat shielded by the company. If you didn't do a great job, your manager caught flak. Or the operator caught flak. Or your company suffered because the customer simply did not return. Oh sure, it may have filtered down to you in the form of a "you screwed up" meeting, but for the most part, you were shielded from the immediate effects of your actions.

In your own business, there is *no place to hide*. If you do a poor job, not only will you know about it, but your wallet or pocketbook will immediately feel the effects. Poor work, or even just "decent" work, will catch up to you. In short, your work has to be nothing short of spectacular.

Do you know the classic portrayal of an artist/computer programmer/inventor — who painstakingly burns the midnight oil to create the perfect piece of work? For the most part, that has to be you. That's why when talking about starting a business, the classic "do something you love" is so paramount. If you don't like the work you are doing enough to do an exceptional job, it will be harder to succeed in business. That's why so many work-at-home schemes like envelope stuffing fail. It's not something most people put on their "life's dreams" lists.

If you start a home-based business solely to make money, that venture is also likely to

fail. Your reasons for wanting to start a home-based business have to be *more* than that — you have to like your work enough to *want* to do a good job.

Throughout this book, I mention many different home-based businesses. Most of these things involve work that people would *want* to start a business in: someone who likes web design opening a web design business; a carpenter striking out on his or her own; or someone who likes kids opening a daycare.

However, I also mentioned businesses such as data entry or medical billing. There is definitely a need for these sorts of businesses, but before you start a data entry business, or try to get into medical billing, do yourself a favor and make an honest assessment of your motivations. Is this something you are really going to *want* to do, day in and day out? Or is your business simply a way to be home when the school bus arrives? I'm not saying you can't succeed with the latter reason (indeed, it's a perfectly viable reason), but I just want to caution you a bit — you probably will need to focus a little more on doing a good job than someone for whom the work is something they love doing.

I'm a writer; I love to write. Everything I write — everything — is the best writing I'm capable of for that topic on that day. If I won a million dollars, I'd still write in some capacity, at the same level of expertise. I might not do it exactly as I do it now, but some form of writing will always be in my life.

Do you think a data entry person or a medical transcriptionist who won a few million dollars would continue with their work? Of course not. So that person is going to have to be *more conscious* of doing good work. It can be done — in fact, I've known a few exceptionally good data entry people.

Of course, quality of work is not the only aspect of running a successful home-based business. Here are several other areas where you really need to stand out:

- **Be accessible**

  How accessible are you? Can clients easily contact you? This is very important for a home-based business. If you are not easily reachable, it conveys the message that you are hiding something.

- **Deal with unpleasant situations**

  There will be exceptions, but for the most part, every unpleasant situation, whether it's your fault or not, needs to be resolved to the customer's satisfaction. And then some.

- **Follow through on all advertised claims**

  You'd be surprised how many businesspeople who advertise "no job too small" don't actually want to do small jobs. Only promise to deliver what you can and *will* deliver.

- **Respond to messages**

  This is another point I want to make about accessibility. Do you respond to messages promptly? Messages need to be responded to within 24 business hours, maximum. The sooner the better; same day is always admirable. (My late Friday messages are sometimes returned Monday. It depends on the client.)

Many contractors, plumbers, and other professional tradespeople have a terrible reputation in this regard, and for the most part, if my personal experience is any indication, it's fairly well earned. Why returning messages is a problem for these professions, I'll never know.

A contractor and/or tradesperson who responds to messages is so rare that he or she will have a *huge* marketing edge over the competition. Please understand that I mean no insult to these trades. I'm merely pointing out that I've hired tradespeople solely because they were the only ones to return my messages.

If you are too busy with work to respond to messages, consider that the person calling might not need you until the winter (or whenever your slow time is), but wants to reserve that time now.

Also, if you are too busy to respond to your messages, it may be an indication that you need to hire some help.

- **Be on time, all the time**

  I cannot count the number of times I've "fired" a contractor or a tree pruner because he or she wasn't on time. To me, not being on time, and not calling me to tell me, is pretty well unforgivable. Okay, you are excused if the bridge collapsed, or gaping holes in the earth opened up in front of you. But that's about it.

Seriously, everyone understands that unforeseen things happen, but if at all possible, you really need to call if you're not going to be able to keep an appointment (within reason — say an hour). It's simply not that hard to do.

If you're someone who just can't seem to do things on time, you're going to have a hard time in business. There is no magic cure. Learn to respect other people's time and schedule your life accordingly. Especially if they are paying you.

- **Follow up when you say you will**

If I say I'm going to call you next Tuesday at noon, your phone will ring next Tuesday at noon. Not at 11. Not at one. Noon. Just like I said. And yes, I'm aware of time zone differences.

My point is, you can set your clock by me — I'm someone who can be counted on to follow up when I say I will.

And to me, there is no excuse — none — for not doing things on time. Why people say things like "I'll get it to you by Tuesday" and then don't do it is beyond me. But millions of people do just that. I have to tell you, that wears thin very, very fast. And it's not going to help you in business.

Be someone who can be counted on to actually follow through. It certainly helps me in my business. I get positive comments on my follow-through all the time.

- **Be someone who gets things done**

You will never go broke if you are a person who can say, "I'll take care of it" and then *actually take care of it*. No excuses. *Just get it done.*

People who can get things done are very rare. The world is full of average people. Be well above average, and it will be one of the biggest edges you'll have in business.

Chapter 20

SOME FINAL TIPS TO HELP YOUR BUSINESS MIND STAY SHARP

In this final part of the Mind section, I'm going to give you a few pieces of advice that I hope you will find helpful. These pointers have all served me very well over the years:

- **Get up at the same time every day and establish a routine**

  Notice I didn't say "get up early." That's because you may not need to. I work best at night (I'm typing these words at 11:49 on a Sunday night), so I choose to work at that time. My time to wake up is a relaxed 9:07 a.m. However, I do wake up at the same time every workday. I have established a comfortable routine, and it helps keep me on track. Not waking up at the same time every day makes everything in your life

  wildly inconsistent, and means your work schedule is inconsistent as well. I might sleep in a bit on weekends, but my workweek routine is pretty strict. I find it helps business a lot.

- **Choose specific times of the day to read, listen to, and respond to messages**

  One of the big problems with a home-based business is the number of rabbit holes you can go down. Here I am, working on something important for Client A, and in comes an email from a Client B. The email states he has a problem. I read the email, get stressed over the problem, get in touch with Client B to solve it, it takes longer than I anticipated … meanwhile, what about Client A?

The day would have gone so much better if I had finished Client A's work before even reading my email. Then I wouldn't have gotten involved with Client B until later. Client B would have been just as happy if I read his email three hours from now and then solved the problem.

Now, I check my email every three hours. This means I check it three times during a business day. A response within three hours should be fast enough for anyone, and it allows me to get work done.

- **Invoice twice a month**

Not only does this make invoicing a breeze (because you don't have to do it daily or weekly), it ensures a nice cash flow (well, as nice as possible).

- **Exercise**

I'm not kidding. Walk every day. Or hit the treadmill. (I do both, depending on the weather. I also lift weights.) If you wish, go to the gym. Exercise gets you moving, gets your blood flowing, and also helps clear your head. The benefits go way beyond weight control.

- **Get a pet**

If you are going to be in your home all day on the computer, get an office cat or dog (I have both). Or an office iguana. Or even an office cactus (which requires very little work, but is also pretty boring). The lack of coworkers can be a little stifling; a pet helps in that regard. It also

makes me truly feel like the boss, as the dogs listen to pretty much everything I say. (I'll admit I can *forget* about asking the cat to do *anything*.)

- **Take time off**

There is no sense in having a home-based business if you are not going to enjoy the fruits of your labor. I advocate working hard, but I also advocate a healthy dose of time off. Working for yourself in a home-based business is much harder than working a job, so you should eventually get *more* vacation than if you had a job (if you can reasonably afford to). In the beginning, start with a few long weekends, and take it from there. It's very easy to get caught up in working too much. Make sure you stop and take a deep breath every now and again.

- **Give yourself a holiday bonus**

If your payroll can afford it, go ahead and give yourself a nice holiday bonus (make sure you report this as income, of course). My wife handles all the accounting for our business, and she decided one year that I should get a bonus. Since she gets one from her job, she felt bad that I didn't get one from the business. When she surprised me with that first holiday bonus from the company, you have no idea how good I felt. It wasn't much, several hundred dollars, but it made me feel so good, and so appreciated. It's now a tradition for me to get a bonus (as long as the company can afford it, of course), and it never ceases to make me feel like a million bucks.

Part 2
BODY

Chapter 21

HOW MUCH MONEY YOU'LL NEED TO START YOUR BUSINESS

I'm not going to kid you — you are going to need some money to start your business. There's no way around this fact.

I know there are all sorts of stories about companies that were "started from scratch in a garage," but they won't apply to you. For starters, the garages in most of these stories were probably of the three-car variety and likely housed Mercedes and BMWs. Starting a business from scratch in such a garage is easy. The "scratch" in question is what Dad doesn't want you to do to the luxury car when you make room for your cute little side venture.

Since it is unlikely the above situation will apply to you, you will need some money to start your business. Exactly how much you need will depend on your individual circumstances, but I'm going to go over the basics. There's also a Start-Up Expense Worksheet on the CD that came with this book.

Immediate Income? Not Likely

If at all possible, do not start your business hoping to get a full-time income from it right away. Even businesses that succeed very seldom generate full-time incomes right away.

I made this mistake once. I *needed* a full-time income when I started my first business. However, this business did not produce a full-time income right away, and the lack of income made me do all kinds of dumb things (painfully described in this book).

I don't care whether you use savings, start the business part time, take a loan, have your spouse work full time and support you, or even use credit cards to float yourself for a while — almost anything is preferable to *needing* a full-time income right from the beginning. That is the root cause of many of the mistakes and pitfalls I outline in this book.

The number one reason why businesses fail is because they are underfunded. You simply cannot start with nothing *or* with the requirement of a full-time income right away. It almost never works. Some of the following advice might seem stern — it's meant to be. Far too many people start a business thinking, "I don't need X right away." That attitude is another big reason why so many home-based businesses fail.

I am going to assume you are starting on a shoestring, but certain things are essential.

Start-Up Expenses

I will be going into more detail later on about the items I talk about in this section:

- Chapter 26 — insurance
- Chapter 27 — home offices
- Chapter 28 — business cards
- Chapter 29 — telephones
- Chapter 31 — computers and software
- Chapters 33 and 36 — advertising
- Chapter 34 — website hosting

Licenses and the business filing fee

You will need to pay a small fee to file your business name, and if the type of business you are going into needs any sort of licensing (for example, as an electrician), you'll need to get that too. Let's budget high and allocate $100.

A functional office/desk and a filing system

Depending on your business, you can simply have a desk in the corner, or an actual office. I will assume that most of you already have something that can be used for this. Even a table works fine. I myself work on a large "table" held up by two short filing cabinets — I like a lot of room, so this affords me more room than a typical desk. Remember, we're going "shoestring" here — you can buy a fancy desk later when you're doing well. Hey, I'm doing fine and I haven't bought a desk yet — I like the big table setup that I have.

Almost any business will need to keep paper records. You can buy a plastic filing box, or you can opt for a real filing cabinet. I recommend the latter. They are very affordable and incredibly functional, and nothing makes you feel quite like you are actually *in* business than having a real filing cabinet with files in it.

Let's budget $300 for a desk, filing system, file folders, paper, assorted pens, paperclips, and other office supplies.

A computer, a printer, and an Internet connection

This is a no-brainer, but you'd be surprised at the number of people who think that a computer is not a necessary part of running a home-based business. You will need a computer to do your bookkeeping, burn backup CDs, update your website, and contact your customers via email.

You will need an online connection. Woe to the businesspeople who think that they don't need email. You can get away with dial-up, but I suggest you splurge and go for a broadband connection.

I recommend that if you are going to do a significant amount of computer-related work, you have a dedicated business computer. So the computer expense for this section is optional: $1,000 for a computer and printer and a few months of Internet service.

Software

If you can afford it and are going into business full time, I suggest purchasing good accounting software. Ask your accountant which type he or she would like you to use. (Most accountants will take your year-end file and work from that, so they may have a suggestion as to which type to buy.)

In addition, if you are going to be doing anything other than basic computer work, you will probably need an "office suite" of common programs. The day someone sends you an MS Word document that you can't open is the day you have to go buy MS Word (or at least download compatible software such as OpenOffice). Don't wait until that time. If you will be exchanging files with clients/suppliers/etc., get an office suite.

Estimated software expense (optional): $600.

A business bank account

Yes, you'll need one. Business-related items going through your personal checking account is a tax nightmare waiting to happen, and it also looks unprofessional.

Let's budget $150 for a deposit to get the account open, and $50 for checks: $200 total.

A separate telephone line and a business phone

When I'm calling to have a job done and a child answers the phone (or if someone just says "hello"), I usually hang up. Maybe that's hard-hearted of me, but I simply feel that I haven't called a real business. It never fails to amaze me how many home-based businesses use their regular phone for business purposes. Don't fool around with this — in the grand scheme of things, it's very inexpensive to have a second phone line. Answer it with your name or company name so people know exactly who they have reached.

Let's budget $50 per month for three months of phone service: $150. Buy yourself a decent phone, too, with a digital answering service: $100. A good, solid phone is another one of those things that will make you feel like you are really in business.

Total phone expense: $250.

Website/email/web hosting

For every type of business, I recommend you get a domain name and have a basic website, one page long at the very least. Let's budget $200 for domain name registration and a year's worth of web hosting/email service.

Business cards

In almost all cases, you will need them. Let's budget $100.

Advertising

This is likely the largest initial expense you will have. You must advertise right from day one, no matter what business you are in. Buy online advertising, get into the phone book, do a direct mailing — whatever — but you will almost always have to advertise. Even if your advertising is you going door-to-door (or business to business), that's still considered "advertising" that must be paid for. (And gas isn't cheap.)

Let's pause a moment and talk about how vitally important advertising is. No business I know has survived without advertising.

There's no dodging it, and you cannot put it off. For example, if you want to start a carpentry business, you need to get a Yellow Pages ad in the next phone book. If you want to start an online web design business, you need an ad on search engines (and probably local advertising as well).

The sole exceptions to advertising right away are if you start your business part time or start off with one big client who will pay the bills for the first few months. Then maybe you can put off advertising for a bit — but even then, if you don't have a contract with this client and they decide to get rid of you, you're sunk.

Advertising costs will vary, but let's budget $500 to $1,000 for the first three months.

Insurance

Most businesses will need some type of liability or "errors and omissions" insurance. Liability insurance is optional, but if you need it, let's budget $500 to get you started.

Totaling the expenses

Let's tack on another $200 for miscellaneous items just to be safe. So let's total up all the expenses:

Filing fee	$100
Basic office supplies	$300
Computer/Internet (optional — only if needed)	$1,000
Software (optional — only if needed)	$600
Business bank account	$200
Business telephone	$250
Website/domain name/email	$200
Business cards	$100
Initial advertising	$500–$1,000
Insurance (optional — only if needed)	$500
Miscellaneous	$200
TOTAL (excluding optional items)	$1,850–$2,350
TOTAL (with optional items)	$3,950–$4,450

So, we have essentially a minimum of almost $1,900. This is hardly starting on a shoestring, huh? And this assumes you provide your own tools, etc. However, I do not recommend starting any business with one dime less than what I've outlined above. And this is a short, bare-bones list.

The simple truth is, if you want people to pay you for anything, you have to project a certain image. And having family members answer business calls with "hello" is not the image a business should be projecting. Handing out cheap, homemade business cards or brochures says either "we're new at this" or "we don't expect to be around very long, so why waste money on this venture?" Not being able to open an MS Word document somebody sent you makes you difficult to work with, as your client has to go to the trouble to get you the information in a form you can open. You don't want to project that image.

Now, having this amount of start-up money does not guarantee success, but it will realistically get almost any home-based business off the ground. If you don't have (or can't raise) this fairly small amount of money, you likely aren't going very far.

Now, obviously, I am leaving out a few big things. If you want to start a plumbing/contracting/tradesperson business, you will probably want/need a pickup truck or a van and some tools. If you want to start a business like mine where your client base finds you online, you need a professional website made, not just one page. But since those situations are both unique to the particular business (not to mention pretty obvious), I'm not including them here.

Chapter 22

OUTSIDE MONEY AND FUNDING (DON'T EXPECT ANY)

Start-up money, in the form of grants and loans, is a huge industry. Every year, millions and millions of dollars are exchanged over elegant tax-deductible lunches, all involving the start-up and/or expansion of businesses.

Not your business, however. Your home-based venture is not likely to see a dime.

I don't mean to be discouraging, but I'm not here to pump you with bad information. The simple truth is, the chance of your home-based enterprise getting funded by a grant or, in the US, an SBA-backed loan is almost zero. (SBA is the Small Business Administration arm of the government.)

The types of businesses that get money are usually established entities that have some collateral and can prove that the money will be used to make more money. This means a proven profit (or at the least a prior track record in making a profit) will almost certainly have to exist. But, to be fair, let's tackle this mystical "outside money" issue head on.

Grants

Being a business writer, I get plenty of emails from start-up entrepreneurs looking for me to write them a proposal to get their business "a grant." My standard answer is, "Okay, exactly *who* are you are asking for the grant? I need to know so I can tailor the proposal to their particular specifications."

In over 500 exchanges, I have never *once* received a clear answer to this question. The usual answer is, "I don't know — I just want to get a grant."

Because I'm in business, I have to be polite and professional, but I want nothing more than to tell these people they'd have a better chance of asking the tooth fairy for money (or Mom and Dad — it's the same thing, if you think about it).

For some reason, people seem to have this belief that there's a huge pile of free money, *just waiting for them*. They think the government is just dying to have people start a home-based business, and is giving away money.

Why do people believe this? Is it because of the crazy guys on late-night TV?

I know the nutty guys on TV say there are all sorts of government programs and a big pile of "hidden money" out there, just waiting for you. And like most claims, no matter how outrageous, there could be a kernel of truth in the midst of all the hype. There probably *are* some oddball and obscure funding programs out there. But, in my experience, in almost all cases the funding is usually reserved for heavy-duty research of new technologies or whatnot — it's very, very unlikely to be earmarked for you.

So I'm sorry to tell you this, but it's very probable that there isn't going to be any free money given to you to start your home-based business. Even if you are a woman. (For some reason, there's also this belief that the government just gives money to any woman who wants to start a business. This just isn't so.)

Think about this logically for a second. I've seen these commercials — they involve oddly dressed people yelling and screaming that the government has all kinds of grants for you to start a business while something like "Free Money" flashes on the screen.

Let me repeat this one more time for effect: Imagine a commercial with a man wearing crazy clothes, and he's yelling and screaming that there's a big pile of money waiting for you. While he's doing this, big letters flash on the screen saying, "FREE MONEY — CALL NOW."

Wow … Just wow.

I mean, can we *possibly* get *any* more over the top than this? Is there anything MORE too-good-to-be-true than advertising FREE MONEY!? It's not even "buy one get one free." Heck, it's not even "buy one get ten free, plus a bowl of soup." It's WAY MORE than that — it's FREE MONEY!!!

Now, normally, people would scoff at this notion. But then the caveat pops up on the screen — "Government Programs." All of a sudden, by just saying those two words, people think it's actually true. They figure if the government will fund research on things like worm reproduction, they'll certainly fund *their* business.

I'm here to tell you they probably won't. It basically boils down to this: In the eyes of the government, worm reproduction is *way* more important than anything your business would do. But you already suspected that, I'm sure.

The truth is, despite whatever programs are out there, there will almost certainly be no grant money for you to start your business. Now if you really think I'm wrong, and that you can indeed get FREE MONEY, by all means, go ahead and buy the "free money book" (it's amusing just to write that) and try to get some.

Don't get your hopes up, though. Nobody I know *ever* got a dime. Ask yourself — do you know anyone who got a federal grant to start a business? Not somebody that you read about, but somebody that you truly know? Who can actually show you a copy of the funding letter/check?

Seriously, the chances of you getting funding from a government grant are almost nil. Time spent trying to get *free money* is time you could be using to do some useful work on your business.

SBA Loans

The SBA isn't likely to help you either. The SBA doesn't really loan money — they serve as a guarantor for bank loans. They generally back loans to entities that have a cash flow and can prove that more money will help them grow (like opening a second location). The truth is they are very unlikely to back, say, a $5,000 loan to start your home-based computer repair or web design business.

This isn't to say the SBA doesn't help people who need money for business; it's just that completely funding small, home-based start-ups like I'm discussing in this book is not something they do. In general terms, if you can't go to the bank and get a regular personal loan for $5,000 (or have access to $5,000 through savings or credit cards), you probably won't be getting an SBA-backed loan either.

However, if you really want to try for an SBA-backed loan, you can. You will have to forgo a lot of what I talk about in this book and prepare a business plan, a projected sales report, a marketing plan, data, stats, etc. Then you will have to convince a bank officer and the SBA that your venture is worth funding. It gives me a headache just to write that — I'd rather just go make money.

There is a *ton* of books and Internet programs out there preying on people's hopes. For $39.99 (or so), they'll lay bare all the secrets to getting SBA money. Be warned: these books are generally worthless.

Venture Capital

What about venture capitalists, or people looking to invest in you? This is always possible, but by and large, a venture capitalist or someone looking to make an investment wants to see that you have a viable enterprise. In general terms, nobody funds an idea and/or a dream, which is usually all a home-based business starts with. Also, the amount of money we're talking about to start your home-based enterprise is likely so small that a venture capitalist won't be interested. Venture capitalists fund million-dollar businesses, not small home-based landscapers.

So Where CAN You Get Money From?

Don't despair — there are places to get money (and as I pointed out in the preceding chapter, most people won't need all that much). Here is a list of possible sources:

1. **Savings**

   If you have some savings and you feel strongly about your business, you could do worse than investing a few bucks in yourself. Also, savings can be used for living expenses if you *do* need a full-time income right away.

I know, it's a no-brainer. But if more people thought of this, fewer people would be stuck with the "no money" problem. Very simple: If you want to start a computer repair business, start doing computer repair on weekends and save the money. When you have enough, start the business full time. If you want to be a carpenter, build decks on weekends and sock away the money.

Yes, it's obvious. Yet, nobody really does it. Instead, they think "Oh, I'll get a grant." No, you won't. Business is tough — work for it.

2. Credit cards/Home equity loans

Risky, of course, but again, if you feel strongly, this kind of money *is* available to just about everyone. I would go so far as to say if you are not willing to stick your neck out some, your moxie probably isn't what it should be. And again, you *can* live on credit for a while until the business grows. Now, is this prudent? That is for you to decide. If you really feel you can make a go of it, it's probably worth the risk (every successful entrepreneur will tell you that some risk is part of the deal).

3. Parents/Relatives

This is a very common place to get some start-up money, especially if you are younger. (My father helped finance my first venture with a $5,000 loan. I failed, but we had a payment schedule, and I stayed on it.) There is risk involved here — not paying back a personal loan from a parent or relative can damage relationships, and the effects can last years. If you don't pay the credit card company — and I don't recommend doing that, mind you — the owner probably won't show up at your door. But if you don't pay back Aunt Jenny, well, let's just say Aunt Jenny is going to be around. And she's nasty when she's angry, with that cane and all. Remember that.

So if you accept a loan from a family member or friend, be clear on what the terms are. Is it a loan or a gift? If it's a loan, a strict repayment schedule is an absolute must — go as far as to make loan coupons with dates. This small step will alleviate a lot of heartache and problems later on.

Chapter 23

ACCOUNTING AND TAXES

There's nothing tricky or profound in this chapter — just some plain-Jane, somewhat stern advice. I say stern, because most everything I'm going to say about accounting and taxes is on the up-and-up, and assumes you will be as well. I am not a fan of playing little games with money, hiding some here, not reporting that, etc. So there are really only a few things we need to go over. The upside to this is if you listen to me, you very likely will avoid any tax or accounting troubles.

The following are my three pieces of advice on this subject:

1. Hire an accountant.

2. Keep good records and receipts.

3. Pay your taxes. No games, no funny business — just report all of your income and pay the taxes you're supposed to.

Let's take a closer look at each of these.

Hire an Accountant

It amazes me that many small business-people feel an accountant is too expensive. They'd rather risk navigating the minefield of taxes themselves (or rely on a friend who "knows taxes") than simply pay a few hundred dollars to a professional to do it.

Listen to me very carefully: For most home-based businesses, paying an accountant will almost always pay for itself.

The IRS rules about taxes, income, and deductions change almost yearly, and your accountant knows them all. I had no idea how many business expenses I was incurring that I was allowed to legitimately deduct until my accountant pointed them out to me. I simply can't keep up with what the IRS allows (and what they don't allow). So I rely on my accountant.

The same is true in Canada. Canada Revenue Agency (CRA) rules change frequently, and an accountant can best advise you on allowable deductions for a home-based business.

I don't mean a tax preparation service; I mean a real accountant. One who understands your business and watches it grow. I've used my accountant since I began my current business, and my wife and I have gone from a sole proprietorship to a corporation. Our income has tripled, and now we have requirements such as quarterly IRS payments and weekly payroll. Our accountant held our hand the entire way. He recommended and even showed us how to use the accounting software so he could take our year-end file and make sense of it. It's a very elegant process, as a matter of fact. And to be perfectly honest, our accountant costs way less than 1 percent of our overall income — to keep the other 99 percent straight. I call that a bargain.

Successful businesses use accountants. It's just that simple.

Keep Good Records and Receipts

Keep a receipt for *everything*. There are many, many things that you may not realize are business expenses, yet they are. Do you have clients coming to your house? Some of your home expenses are likely partially tax deductible. Do you live in a snowy place? Then your snowblower is likely at least partially tax deductible. Do you use the Internet for your business? That expense is likely partially deductible.

Of course, your accountant will have the final say on what you can claim and what you cannot (sadly, the IRS and CRA won't buy "but Dan said I could deduct the Internet expense …"), and your receipts provide your accountant with what you bought and/or spent on business.

So save ALL RECEIPTS. File them into different categories: house expenses, clothing, medical, obvious business expenses, maintenance, etc. If you can, use a credit card for everything even remotely business related — this gives you a nice record to fall back on. (Of course, make sure you pay the balance monthly.) Keep orderly receipts, total them up, and go over it all with your accountant to determine which ones are legitimate expenses.

If you have a true home office, let your accountant know, and keep receipts for everything you do to it. Now, I know a lot of people are afraid of this because of the old "isn't a home office an audit red flag?" Well, maybe it is (although I think it's a myth), but even *if* it is true, you will have nothing to fear from an audit if you do everything on the up-and-up.

Pay Your Taxes

I'm going to make this very simple: Just pay your taxes. No hiding money, no not-reporting income. Just report what you make, keep honest books, and pay what you owe — you'll have nothing to worry about then. Just do it.

I've known all kinds of people who have tried to cheat on taxes, and almost all of them ended up having tax trouble at one time or another. Just do things right, and you'll have no tax troubles.

Truth be told, the government *wants* you to have a successful business. Well, maybe not everyone in the government. I'm sure Marge, the surly desk clerk at your local government office, doesn't really care if you succeed or not. In fact, all she really cares about is putting up with two more years of this @#$%, because then she'll have her twenty in. But until that time, she'll be ready to serve you with that ever-so-slight amount of uncaring scorn that makes government offices such a joy to visit.

But on the whole, yes, the government wants you to succeed. The tax department has all kinds of legitimate deductions they are perfectly happy to give you. But the caveat is you do have to pay taxes on what you earn.

Now, I realize many people like to be paid cash, because then they don't feel they have to report it. I can't count the number of times I've heard something like, "Pay me cash and I'll charge you less."

If you do this, I'm going to tell you to stop. Do you know why? Well, first because it's really bad and I'm trying to score points with the tax department. But the bigger reason is that you have no idea what your customer will do afterwards.

Say your customer ends up not being happy with your work and decides to be a jerk and report you. It *could* happen. Disgruntled ex-spouses also *love* to report you for being a tax cheat.

Secondly, often the work you did for people will be tax deductible by them. Suppose your customer reports the work you did as a deduction? Suppose he or she gets audited and produces the receipt you wrote for the payment? You didn't report that income … Trust me, uncaring Marge no longer works for the IRS. Instead, Irwin, the guy who was the hall monitor in school and always reminded the teacher to give homework, works there now. Irwin will take great interest in your situation.

It's so much easier to just report your income and pay your taxes. It's fair, and it's the law.

Two Last Things on Taxes

Tax refunds

We're all conditioned to expect a tax refund every year. We like the tax refund — a lot, in fact. When we fill out our tax form at work, we even tell the government: "Here, take MORE than you need. Just spend it wisely, and give the overpayment back to me at the end of the year." And if you are still working full time, or have a spouse who is working, your home-based business may not change that — at least in the very beginning.

However, if you make any decent amount of money in your home-based business, getting a refund will almost certainly become a distant memory. You will probably owe money at tax time — which is all the more reason to hire an accountant. Not only can an accountant likely lessen the blow because he or she knows more than you do about deductions, he or she can also help prepare you for the inevitability of owing money — so you're not shocked at year-end.

I know for myself, I will never, ever see another tax refund. Know what? I'm doing fine, and I'm not complaining. Look at the big picture and your overall income, and forget trying to work the numbers so you still get a tax refund.

Write-offs

It's my opinion that many people are confused about the whole "write-off" thing. That's because there seems to be a general consensus that "writing something off" means it's free. For example, when I bought a new printer, a non-business-owning friend said, "Oh, you're lucky — you can just write that off." I asked him why that was "lucky," and he replied, "Well, you don't really pay for it."

I don't? Really??

After I stopped laughing, I explained to him what a write-off generally was.

A write-off is simply a business expense. Here's an easy example: Say my printer cost $300 and this was my only business expense for the year. And let's say my business made $50,000 for the year.

Now, normally, I would pay taxes on $50,000. But because I had a $300 business expense, my business *really* only made $49,700. So instead of paying taxes on $50,000, I only have to pay tax on $49,700. So I don't "save" the actual money I write off — just the *tax* I would have paid on it.

Now, let's assume a simple tax rate of 20 percent. I don't have to pay the 20 percent tax on that $300 write-off. Meaning I saved $60.

So the bottom line is this: Buying that printer for my business saved me $60 in taxes. I still spent the $300, but I paid $60 less in taxes. While this makes business expenses a little easier to swallow, this is hardly "not paying for it." (And if the printer is used only partly for the business and partly for personal use, the tax saving will be even less.)

I just wanted to clear up this little issue, because a lot of people seem to think small businesspeople get all sorts of stuff for free. Well, I'm sorry to say, we don't. That means if one of your reasons to own a business is the mountains of free merchandise you are expecting, I'm telling you that you will be very disappointed. You may as well envision "mountains of free merchandise delivered by scantily clad models floating on a river of chocolate" for all the good it'll do you.

Chapter 24

POLICIES AND FORMS (YES, YOU NEED THESE, AND THEY AREN'T AS BORING AS YOU THINK)

Policies and forms don't have to be a dull, dry part of your business. They can be sexy, exciting, and dynamic — in short, they can be an integral part of your overall marketing efforts.

Well, maybe those adjectives are a little extreme. No matter how you dress it up, your proposal form will never be as sexy or as well received as, say, the Victoria's Secret catalog. However, it *can* be slightly more dynamic than *Ed's Big Book of Seeds*.

My point is, your invoices, proposal forms, and written policies do *not* have to be run of the mill. In fact, they can actually help you market your business and increase sales.

The Forms You Need

I have to admit, I keep things simple. I use three basic forms in my business: (They are all on the CD that comes with this book.)

- **Proposal/Quote form**

  This is *the* form — the bread and butter. This is the first form a client gets from me. After the client and I have emailed and/or talked, this form spells out the job, asks for a deposit, and lists my terms and conditions (which are decidedly nonlegalese).

- **The client sheet**

  After a client has secured my services, they get a client sheet to fill out and send back to me. This sheet contains all vital client information, and asks specific questions pertaining to the project.

- **The invoice**

    After the job is done, I send the client an invoice for the balance due.

Let's look at each of these a little more closely.

The Proposal Form

I used to be like every other businessperson — I used generic forms. I used whatever template MS Word had; slapped my name onto it; and that was my proposal/quote form. You likely do the same (or plan to do the same). Nothing wrong with that.

However, I'm a writer, and I understand how words have the power to motivate certain behaviors. One day, I was looking at my proposal form, and I realized what a poor job it did of selling my service.

Here was a form that I sent to a customer after I spoke to him or her. It contained the job, the price, the deposit requirement, etc. It also contained some legal jargon. And that's about all it contained. A pretty standard proposal/quote form.

Now understand the thought process here. Once this form is in my prospective client's hands, *it is the LAST piece of ammunition I have left in my sales arsenal.* I may have done a good job of closing the deal in person or on the phone, but if the customer had any lingering doubt or was teetering in any way, this form was all he or she had. In addition, if the person I closed with had to discuss the project with anyone — a committee, a boss, a spouse (same thing) —

this form was what they brought them. And that second person (or committee) didn't hear my sales pitch — all they had was a cold, hard quote form. Ugh.

So, being a writer, I tweaked my proposal form. I really only added a little bit. I added a short passage about what the price includes (the price includes *everything* — no hidden charges), and then I added a closing statement as to why good writing is worth the money. I also added that a writing revision is included in the price, in case a client is not happy with my services.

Know what happened? My closing rate went up considerably. Typically, I closed with about half the people I sent my proposal to. The other half just didn't use me for whatever reason. Once I changed my proposal form to portray *better value*, instead of closing with 50 percent of the people I sent it to, I started closing with about 75 percent.

Let's make no mistake: This is a HUGE, absolutely monumental change. All from a few simple words on a document that most people don't even give a second thought to. (By the way, I call it a proposal form — you may call it a quote form, an estimate sheet, whatever.)

So I learned something valuable — your proposal form should sell. Period. Sample 1 illustrates what I'm talking about.

I then go on to list the time frames, and get into the deposit requirements, the fine print, the revision statement (which is my guarantee), and so on. A complete form is provided on the CD.

Notice the small "this total includes" sales statement after the space for the price. This seemingly small thing made a *huge* difference in my closing rate.

PROPOSAL FORM

logo	**Your Company Name** Address 1 Address 2 Your name and your title	Phone (555) 555-5555 Fax (555) 555-5555 Website: www.yourwebsite.com Email: youremail@yourwebsite.com

Proposal

Prepared For:

Proposal Date:

Estimated Project Start Date:

Project Description:

Estimated Total: $

This total includes *everything* for the above project as described — all research, brainstorming, editing, proofreading, minor expenses, applicable taxes, and (of course) great writing are all included in the price.

I then finish with a small statement that wraps things up. Sample 2 shows the last thing the clients read on my proposal form.

The Client Sheet

Every piece of contact information is recorded on the client sheet. I send this to my client after he or she has secured my services and gives me a deposit. This is the main form in a client's file. I keep my files on computer and don't print them out; you might do it differently. Either way, it's *the* form you consult when you need to contact the client, etc. Included on my client sheet is all contact information, the names of everyone I'll be dealing with, etc.

Also included are questions/details pertaining to the project I am working on for the client. For example, right on my client sheet, I ask about their business that I'm writing about, links to competing websites, the tone they wish me to use, what results they are expecting from my writing, etc. Your client sheet may have other info. If you're running a daycare, perhaps it will list a child's allergies. If you're a plumber, perhaps you want to note if the customer has a septic tank or uses the town sewer. Add anything you can think of that might be useful.

The Invoice

There isn't much to say about the invoice. You've seen one, you've seen them all. Be sure to thank the client for their business, and include all of your contact information. I also put a link to my website payment

SAMPLE 2
CLOSING STATEMENT ON PROPOSAL

The Cost of Good Writing

Good writing should earn you back every penny you spend on it, and then some. **In other words, good writing costs you nothing, and instead MAKES you money.**

When your written communications are clear and compelling, they get across what you intended to get across, and persuade an action from your reader. **Good writing is worth every penny.**

In reality, it's writing that doesn't get read that costs you money.

---

page, letting the client know they can easily pay me online via credit card.

About Legalese

I've seen competitors and colleagues use complicated, cold "work agreements" that spell everything out to the last detail. If you think you need this kind of document, get one made by a lawyer (or download one from one of a million do-it-yourself legal services online).

However, I don't bother with these. Maybe I'm dumb (ya think?), but *I don't get too wrapped up in legalese.*

First of all, legalese that protects you in ironclad terms tends to scare clients. I tried it. No client would sign my work agreement that said I could sue them in my county for nonpayment (which is a very common clause in work agreements).

I'm in favor of spelling out important things, like what the project is, when it's going to be completed, how much it will cost, etc. I'm not much of a fan of spelling out where the lawsuit will take place — that just puts a cloud over everything.

It has been my experience that almost all clients pay, and if they don't, you never will see a dime anyway, legalese or not. I found the best "protection" I could possibly have is getting a solid deposit, and doing good work so they would *want* my services again. Now, this could change if I start doing $50,000-dollar projects on a regular basis. I may then want more legal protection (and if you're in that situation, you might too). But I find it a little silly to get ironclad "here's where the lawsuit will take place" statements on a $2,500-dollar job.

Time for the disclaimer again: I'm not a lawyer. The preceding is my opinion. Use my advice at your own risk.

Policies and Guarantees

Let's talk about policies and guarantees for a second. Policies first.

To begin, I realize not every business will need written policies, but most *should* have them. Almost every business should have a defined, consistent way of handling things, and a written statement about how they go about doing business. And your customers should be aware of these policies.

For example, are deposits refundable? What happens if you can't perform the job by the agreed-upon time — will you call? What if you own a daycare, and an emergency happens and you have to close for a day? It is a good idea to spell out what happens in each of these instances. Many of your policies can go right on your quote form.

Not only does having clearly defined policies help out when things go wrong, it also gives you a chance to make a GREAT impression on clients. For example, almost every business should have a clear statement about when the work mentioned on the quote form will start. This is a great selling tool, as it not only tells clients what to expect, but it can really set you apart. For example, a contractor can state on the quote form: "We will start your project on the date specified on our proposal. However, emergencies and weather can and do affect our business. If for some reason we will not be able to start your project at the date and time specified, we will make every effort to both contact you as soon as possible, and to reschedule work at the earliest possible time."

If a contractor handed me a quote form that included a statement like that, I'd use them forever. Talk about a reassuring professional.

So what are your policies? Do you spell them out? Are customers aware of them? Are you using them to help reassure your customers? You should be.

Now let's discuss guarantees for a second. I realize that not many businesspeople, especially small businesspeople, like guarantees. They think customers will take advantage of them.

I'm here to tell you most won't. Offering a guarantee is an excellent sales tool. If you are willing to stand behind your work, I am much more willing to use your services. For some businesses, a guarantee is straightforward, particularly if you are a tradesperson. In many businesses, a general statement such as, "We guarantee you'll be happy or you get _____ free" is appropriate.

Let me tell you, most people will never take you up on it. (How many times have *you* actually taken someone up on a guarantee?) And the few that do, well, they give you a chance to really shine and solidify their return business — after all, you made it right. And you can always limit the guarantee with words like "reasonable," "normal wear and tear," etc.

My guarantee for my clients is I'll revise what I wrote. One free revision is included, and "at our discretion," I'll revise it again and again. I add "at our discretion" to prevent someone from making me work forever on one project.

Your policies and forms can really be an integral part of your marketing. Pay some attention to them.

Chapter 25

ACCEPTING CREDIT CARDS (YOU MUST, AND IT'S EASIER THAN YOU THINK)

Okay, let's discuss credit cards. I don't mean you using them — I mean you accepting them. In simple terms, you *must* accept credit cards — I don't care what type of business you are in. There are two big reasons for this, one obvious, and one not so obvious.

The obvious reason is we are very quickly moving toward a cashless/paperless society. Many people use very little cash. I know, because my wife and I are two of them. We use our credit cards for almost everything (and we pay the bill in full every month — I don't want to get any financial advisers mad here). It simply allows us to keep better track of what we are spending, and it makes business expenses a breeze to keep

straight. A $10 bill can last for weeks in my wallet.

Offering someone like me a credit card option makes it more convenient for me to pay, simply because I don't carry a lot of cash, and I have not written a check in years. Anything that makes life more convenient for your customers is good. In fact, I use my credit card for all business expenses, including services like carpet cleaning.

The second, not-so-obvious reason for accepting credit cards is that there is an entire segment of the population who uses credit cards not as a convenience, *but as a way of life*. In short, putting something on credit is the only way they can pay for many products or services. While credit counselors deplore this behavior, the simple truth is, it's a fact of life for many, many people. So not taking credit cards shuts you off from countless customers.

For example, I know a couple who chose their daycare provider largely based on the fact that the daycare took credit cards. They pay the daycare provider on credit, make minimum payments to the credit card company throughout the year, and pay it all off with every tax refund. Hey, it works for them.

Regardless of whether this is a prudent financial strategy or not, my concern is if you ran a daycare and you didn't take credit cards, *you'd be shutting yourself off from this couple's business*. Why would you shut yourself off from any client?

Many years ago, right after I went broke in my first business, if you didn't take credit cards, you'd have shut yourself off from *me* (not that that would have been a terrible thing at that time, mind you). In short, I couldn't afford *anything* unless Uncle Visa bought it for me. I based a ton of buying decisions solely on whether the Visa logo was being displayed.

There's also the emergency factor to consider. For example, can you imagine an auto repair shop not taking credit cards? They'd go out of business if they didn't. That's because auto repairs are largely unexpected, and a lot of people don't have the cash on hand to pay for them. So they charge it.

But if an auto repair shop uses this reasoning to take credit cards, why wouldn't a plumber? Or an electrician? Or a computer repair specialist?

Or remember in Chapter 22 when I said credit cards were a fine way to fund your initial business expenses? Might that be true of *your* clients as well? I know more than one person who had a business website built on credit.

Or how about a couple not wanting to wait until their tax refund to have a deck built? If they could find a contractor who takes credit cards, they'd do it now. Can *you* be that contractor?

Accepting Credit Cards Is Simple

The Internet has made taking credit cards astonishingly easy for any business. (You do *not* need that little swipe terminal.) All you need to do is go online and do a little research.

I use Skipjack Financial Services, and I also use PayPal (links are on the CD). Skipjack has a neat setup where I direct my clients to a form, and *the client* fills in the amount to pay me. That really helps, because each job is priced differently.

It's very elegant and simple, and with a minimum amount of work, *you* can have a form set up where people go to pay you, too. Instead of handing a customer a paper invoice, you can email them an invoice with your form's link on it.

Yes, this will involve a little bit of work on your end, and you're going to have to get a little comfortable with the Internet, but it's not nearly as complicated as you may think. If you can email photos to someone, you can just as easily email an invoice and get paid by credit card.

You can also use PayPal as a credit card processor. Just go to their website and set up an account. It's extremely simple. Then anyone can pay you with a credit card. You can even make an invoice on PayPal and email it to your client. As an added bonus, at the time of this writing, PayPal is free to set up.

Now, as a disclaimer, I do not have any affiliation with either of these businesses other than I am a customer. Nor am I responsible for anything that happens should you decide to use them. I simply wanted to tell you whose services I use.

Let Me Take a Moment to Dispel a Few Credit Card Myths

- **"My clients don't care about credit cards"**

  Yes, they do. Offer to take them, and you'll be surprised. In addition, it's likely that a lot of your competition *do not* take credit cards. This can be a big advantage for you, and really make your home-based business stand out.

- **"Credit cards are too expensive — they want so much in fees"**

  Nonsense. While it's true that credit card companies (or PayPal) will charge transaction fees, it amounts to next to nothing in the big scheme of things. It's like you waffling over my saying, "Here, see this $100 bill? It's yours, as long as you give me back $10." You will more than make up any fees in added business.

- **"People can dispute credit card transactions if they don't like my work"**

  In all the years I've accepted credit cards, this has not happened once. If you do good work and stand behind it, this won't be a problem.

- **"I need a merchant account, which is impossible to get"**

  Not true anymore. The Internet has changed everything. Go online and do some investigating. Pick a company and make a phone call. Ask questions, and you'll be pleasantly surprised by the answers.

- **"I don't have good credit — how can I accept credit cards?"**

  Most credit card processors don't care how good your credit is or isn't.

There is absolutely no downside — none whatsoever — to you accepting credit cards. You have everything to gain and nothing to lose. In fact, accepting credit cards is something that can really make or break your business.

Let me recap this one more time:

1. **Accepting credit card payments is simple to set up**

   You can either have an online payment form via a regular credit card processor such as Skipjack, or you can simply have a PayPal account. These things are extremely simple to set up. (They are both available in Canada as well.) Either way, the result is the same. Your clients go to a web page to enter in their credit card number and pay you. You don't even need a website, nor do you ever personally handle the client's credit card number.

2. **It's easy for your customer**

All you need to do is give your client the address to your payment web page. You can put the link right on your invoice (like I do — see my sample invoice on the CD). You can even use PayPal to send an invoice via email.

3. **That's it — you get paid**

Your money goes right into your business bank account (if you use a Skipjack-type service) or your Pay-Pal account (which you can then transfer to your bank account).

If you take any time to learn something new about business, this is the one area I'd really recommend investing several hours on. It's simple, and with a little bit of effort, you can really add a huge advantage to your home-based business.

Chapter 26

LAWYERS, ZONING, INSURANCE, AND OTHER BORING THINGS

The easiest way to bore someone to death is to start talking about legal issues, zoning regulations, and insurance. So, since I promised you in the beginning that this book would not be boring, we're going to skim over these with a minimum of fuss. However, I still want you to read this chapter, as this information is important. In fact, ignoring these three vital topics could very well be the dumbest move you make in business. So I'll try to make this as interesting as possible.

Lawyers and Legal Issues

Getting to know a lawyer is one of the more important things you can do. Anyone who can say "I'll call my lawyer" has a distinct advantage over someone who is reduced to

opening the phone book or turning on the TV and picking a lawyer who has an appealing ad. Saying, "Yeah, I'll look for a lawyer" just doesn't have the same impact.

Speaking of which, would you believe there's a law firm in my area that uses the word *shenanigans* in their advertising? As in, "When you contact Ellis Teabags and Partners [*not their real name*], the shenanigans stop." I didn't know people actually used that word. But I digress.

My point is, at some juncture, you will have legal questions regarding your business: Can you legally do this? Can you claim that? Can you get out of this contract? There is no better person to answer these questions than a lawyer. If you don't already know a lawyer, ask around. As a last resort, look in the phone book. Request an hour of consultation time (which you'll pay for, of course). Ask your questions.

Two things will happen: 1) you'll get your legal questions answered by an expert; and 2) you'll get to know a lawyer, and he or she will get to know you. Next time you'll be able to say, "Let me call my lawyer."

Zoning

Zoning could really bite you when you least expect it if you are not careful. Make sure the business you want to start is compliant with local zoning laws. Now, for many businesses, this really isn't a concern. For example, just about anyone can start a home-based Internet-type business (but don't take my word for it — you are responsible for checking).

Of course, there are obvious businesses for which you really need to investigate zoning, such as if you are going to have clients visit your home to do business (like with a daycare, a hair salon, or even a photography studio). You must ensure that your business premises are zoned for such activities.

But even not-so-obvious businesses can encounter problems. For example, is it okay to park a work truck in your driveway? You'd be surprised, but some neighborhoods frown upon vehicles with a company name painted on them parked at houses.

So my advice here is check your local zoning codes (call your local zoning office) and make sure what you want to do is okay.

Insurance

Don't skimp when it comes to insurance. For some home-based businesses, you may need some type of liability insurance. If you do need it, get it.

Any professional trade needs insurance. A daycare needs insurance. In fact, it's likely any business where people visit your home needs insurance. Your homeowner's policy may not cover clients coming to your home to do business. Even when I was a computer programmer, I carried errors and omissions insurance in case my programming fouled up someone's system.

So get the proper insurance. It's the right thing to do, and doing things right is the only way to do business.

One additional word of advice on this: Saying you are "fully insured" when you are not is illegal. I have known guys who do work on the weekends and tell people they are insured when they really aren't. They figure, "Well, I'll be careful, so nothing will happen …" Well, DUH — that's why they call those things where items fall and people lose body parts *accidents*. If you could avoid them 100 percent of the time by being careful, there would be no accidents.

Chapter 27

THE MAKINGS OF A FUNCTIONAL HOME OFFICE

The Basics

I also promised I would not waste a lot of time on home offices, so I won't. First, let's very quickly talk about some basic office machines:

- **Fax machines**

    If you find yourself *sending* a lot of faxes, you probably should buy a fax machine (or an all-in-one machine). But, if you *receive* far more faxes than you send, you can get away with using an online service to receive your faxes. I use one myself (check out www.accessline.com). It's a few bucks a month, I get a local fax number to give to clients, and the service emails me when I get a fax. I go to their site, download the fax, and I'm done. The three times a year I have to *send* a fax, I use a local copy/fax center.

- **Photocopy machine**

    I can't think of many home-based businesses that need a copier at start-up. Okay, maybe if you open an accounting service, you might need one. Many fax machines also masquerade as copiers/printers/scanners, so one of those all-in-one machines might make sense.

- **Computer**

    At the very least, you're going to need to use email and print invoices, so you are going to need a computer. I suggest either having a dedicated business computer, or at least using the adults-only computer in the house.

Don't use the family computer for business if you can avoid it, especially if you have kids. The reason is, every kid I know ends up fouling up the family computer with spyware and viruses by going to game sites, hacking sites, and the never-ending search for porn (which is the number one hobby for teenage boys everywhere). It just doesn't help your business when you send your clients a virus.

- **Telephones**

    Telephones are important enough to warrant their own chapter — see Chapter 29.

- **Desk, chair, file cabinet**

    As I mention in Chapter 21, you will need some kind of desk and filing setup. What form that takes I'll leave up to you.

Now let's move on to the home office itself.

The Three Different Types of Home Offices

There are generally three types of home offices for home-based businesses. They all have different requirements.

The home-based business where you don't do a lot of work *at* home

This would apply to a typical tradesperson, landscaper, etc. Since the work you do is generally outside your home, your home office needs are very, very basic — especially in the beginning. In all honesty, you probably don't need an "office." A filing cabinet, a kitchen table, a phone, and the adults-only computer might be all you need.

You actually do the work at home, but don't see clients there

This is the "classic" work-at-home example. This is what I do, and what anyone working on the computer does.

For this type of business, you are more than likely going to need a real office, *especially* if you do computer-based work. One exception would be if you are making a product in your garage, and spend most of your time there. Then an "office" isn't so important. In fact, if that's your situation, move the computer and phone to the garage and make that your office/workshop.

But for anything else, you are going to need an office. An office that says "work."

To be honest, I could not do my job from a kitchen table. Or from the living room computer. No way, no how. I'm a professional, doing professional work for professional clients. Working on your living room computer is not very professional, and more importantly, it doesn't *feel* very professional.

I know this is of little comfort to someone with nothing *but* the living room computer. But I'm not here to give you bad information — I'm giving it to you straight. If you're going to do the work in your home, on your computer, eight hours a day, get creative and carve yourself out some space. Put some paneling up in the basement or garage and move into there. Or section yourself off a corner of the bedroom. Do whatever it takes to get yourself a dedicated work space.

I know this from experience. I now know that lack of an office is one reason I failed in my Internet advertising/computer business in the mid-'90s. I simply cannot work with someone else in the room watching TV. Most people cannot. They think they can before they actually do it, but it's VERY hard to actually do work from a pure "home" environment.

Space is another issue. With my line of work (writing), I need a lot of space. I have to-do lists, two different trays of paperwork, a white board hanging on the wall, pens, highlighters, two phones, two filing cabinets, etc. Almost any computer-based home-based business will need similar furnishings.

Yes, I know there's a perception that working at home can be done from the kitchen table. This makes for great advertising copy in those get-rich-quick advertisements. But nobody I know ever succeeded in running a real business while waiting for everyone to finish breakfast so they could get to work. Again, the kitchen table is fine for a contractor to do his or her billing twice a month. But for everyday work? No way.

Another important point about having a dedicated office space is that you will be spending a lot of time there. It has to be a place where you feel comfortable *working*. The kitchen is where I go when my wife is cooking; for me, working there doesn't mix well.

I have decorated my home office to the nines. I have it exactly the way I want it, and to be perfectly honest, I *love* working here. I've created myself a wonderful work atmosphere. I have all my business stuff, files and such, but I also have shelves of horror collectibles, posters, owls of all kinds (I really like owls), a laptop computer for backup/traveling, etc. It's a *very* comfortable place, and as a result, I am very happy and comfortable working here. And that attitude and feeling extends to the work I do.

If I were at the kitchen table … well, to be blunt, if I didn't have this office, I probably wouldn't have my own business either.

Now I'm not going to tell you silly things like, "when the door is closed, that means you're working and nobody should bother you." That's nonsense. My wife can talk to me anytime, and if the cat feels the need to be petted (often), by all means, let me know. But the point is, if my wife wants to talk to me, she has to *physically* come to my office. She can't just look up from the newspaper and begin speaking (well, she can, but I won't hear her). And she's pretty good about not interrupting me when I'm working. Good judgment and understanding are better than locked doors.

One last thing on the work-from-home-on-the-computer setup — a nice chair is paramount. Forget the $89 special. As soon as you can afford it, spend a few hundred dollars on a quality chair. You'll be happy you did.

You work at home, and you see clients there

Hair stylist, accountant, portrait studio … all of these lend themselves to clients coming to you. In this case, your office and your work space will likely be merged, and it has to look professional. This type of business really cannot be run in your living room. But you already know this, so we won't elaborate on the obvious. All I need to say is, in addition to your client work space, you'll need a desk/computer/file cabinet setup somewhere in the corner. But for businesses like these, the customer/work area is more important than the desk area.

Chapter 28

BUSINESS CARDS AND BROCHURES

Business Cards

Two points about business cards.

First of all, don't go cheap. Those inkjet business cards that you print yourself just scream bargain basement. A business card is an extension of *both* you and your business — think of it as your calling card.

I'm not saying you have to spend a lot of money, but you should get professionally made business cards from a local printer. Choose a nice color, good-quality paper, and glossy or raised type — we're not looking to "wow" anyone here, but your business card should *never* say "cheap." So get professional cards made.

For tradespeople and service professionals, invest in a few hundred magnetic cards (or sticky magnetic backs for your cards). Yes, people really do put them on the refrigerator. Even if it's only used to hold up little Dorothy's picture of a dog (bird? car? It's hard to tell, really). There are far worse places your business name can be than right in front of a potential customer's eyes.

The second thing about cards is do NOT cram the card full of useless information and silly slogans. Sample 3 is a self-produced card a client asked me to redesign some years ago. The name is changed to protect the guilty.

What a way to confuse the reader and give FAR too much useless information. I have to tell you, my eyes almost started to bleed when he showed me this. And he actually asked me to come up with *another*

Crash McRickety Building Services

Free Estimates
Friendly Service

Crash McRickety - Owner

Call Crash when short on cash!

Knowledgeable
and reliable

* **Fully Insured**
* **No Job Too Small**
* **Quality work at low prices**

New Construction, Small Repairs,
Remodels, and more. Call us for a great price!

201 Main Street
Anytown, US 12345
Phone: 555-555-5555
E-mail: someone@example.com
www.examplewebsitename.com

Serving the area since 1996

---

phrase to cram into the little white space on the bottom right. Isn't that just insane?

Notice that he mentions price and/or cash three times. I'm in favor of mentioning price ZERO times. People who hammer price as a reason to do business with them end up hating the work they do. The funny thing is, he saw himself as a professional builder — a craftsman, if you will — and not some screaming price huckster. He simply thought white space in his card was "wasted space." Not so. White space is good. I told him I'd fix it.

Using the same overall design, I changed his card as shown in Sample 4.

I got rid of useless fluff like "knowledgeable and reliable" and the silly slogan. This gave me the room to add a nice two-line description. I even got in the words "professional craftsmanship," and personalized it to the reader by using the word *your*. This card is much more understated, and far more professional.

This card not only looks better, it actually solves a reader's problem, too. It essentially says that Crash can handle all of your building needs. "Building needs" are exactly what someone calling a builder has. This card is a *much* better representation of the business, and is something Crash would be happy and proud to hand out. Suffice to say, he loved it.

Crash McRickety Building Services

Crash McRickety - Owner

Professional craftsmanship for all of your building needs.
New Construction, Remodels, and Small Repairs.

* Fully Insured
* No Job Too Small
* Free Estimates

Serving the area since 1996

201 Main Street
Anytown, US 12345
Phone: 555-555-5555
E-mail: someone@example.com
www.examplewebsitename.com

The key is to make the business card not do too much. Say what you do, say something nice about yourself, and tell the person reading how to get in touch with you. That's it. Leave "knowledgeable and reliable" out of it.

Brochures

Brochures come in all shapes and sizes. You have your classic trifold, you have that one-page advertisement you see stapled to telephone poles everywhere, and you have the supermarket tear-off sheet, to name a few.

There's really only one thing I can say about brochures: Don't make them yourself. Please?

Just like homemade business cards, homemade brochures send the wrong message. They're great for a teenager who wants to cut lawns or shovel snow, and there is no finer way to advertise a garage or bake sale. But serious businesses don't use these. I would wager that you will do yourself more harm than good with homemade brochures.

I know I mention similar advice in other places in this book, but spending a few dollars on quality brochures is one of the things that separate a successful business from one of the millions that fail.

Chapter 29

THE TELEPHONE

I'm going to tell you to spend some money again. Sorry. (I'll stop soon — I promise!)

Almost all home-based businesses try to save a few bucks on the telephone. This is a bad practice. In reality, a second phone line and a good business phone are not very expensive at all.

So why a second phone line? Don't most phone companies offer a quasi-second line that rings differently? For less money than a full-blown telephone line?

Yeah, they do, and it's exactly what you think it is — it's cheap. Both in price, and in practice. There are two distinct drawbacks to using a "distinct ring" phone line:

1. If the phone is in use by a family member, you can't use the "other" line.

2. Since it's the family phone, some-one will frequently forget that it's the business ring and answer it "hello." Or a child will answer it. That's the kiss of death.

Answering a business line with "hello" makes for a bad first impression. If I call a business and that's what I get, I'm likely to say, "Sorry, wrong number" and hang up.

The same applies if a child answers. A young child answering the phone is cute to only a *very* small circle of relatives. To everyone else, it's mildly annoying. And to clients, it's a major turn-off.

The bottom line: A dedicated business phone line is a must. Oh, you can get away without one — plenty of businesses do. But without question, lack of one will cost you business. Of course, your nonclients won't tell you *why* they didn't call back, or why they hung up — they just won't do business with you. And you will never escape the stigma of not being a "real" business until you get a dedicated business line.

Think of it this way: You are going to have to pay for the long distance calls your business makes anyway, so the only real difference is the basic line charges. We're probably talking less than $50 a month. $50 a month is not worth *one* client getting a negative impression.

Having a dedicated phone line is one of the things that separates a real business from those millions of "in business one day, out of business tomorrow" home-based ventures that get started every year. People doing scrapbooking services don't get a second phone line. Real businesses do. From day one.

Answering the Phone

Answer the phone with either your business name, or, if you do work like I do, you can answer it with your name. But don't answer it with "hello," and don't let other nonbusiness family members answer it.

Messages

I find that a phone with a digital answering machine works nicely. I also subscribe to the phone company's voice-mail service as a backup (for an additional few bucks a month). This way nobody ever gets a busy signal, as the voice mail kicks in when I'm on the phone.

The Phone Itself

If you are on the phone a lot, or you are going to be on the phone while working on the computer, a hands-free headset is a lifesaver. I *love* mine. I put it on my cordless phone, put the phone itself on the desk, and I'm free to work on the computer, go over a website while I have the client on the phone, etc.

The phrase "you get what you pay for" is usually true, but it goes doubly so for phones. In simple terms, cheap phones sound cheap. Buy a nice phone — it will be one of the better business investments you will make.

Chapter 30

VEHICLES

There's not much to say about vehicles in a "here's what you should get" sense. The cars you have are the cars you have, and unless you have a lot of money, you probably aren't buying a new car just for business.

That being said, if you are going to do any type of construction or landscaping work, you will probably need a van or pickup truck. It's very hard to do that type of work for any length of time without one.

However, apart from that, here are a few words of advice about vehicles:

- **Keep them clean**

    If clients will see your vehicle, even if it's just parked in your driveway, it forms an impression. Unfair as it may seem, a clean, well-maintained car says "responsible person"; an unkempt, sloppy car says the opposite. Even an old car can look somewhat decent with a small amount of elbow grease (well, wax).

    If you have a construction-trade or landscaping business (or similar), buy a magnetic sign. You may not have the funds to go for a full "company name" paint job on your vehicle, but a decent-size magnetic sign with your business name and phone number can be had for a few bucks. Well worth it.

- **Keep a mileage log**

  Every mile you drive for business is probably tax deductible (ask your accountant about this). Keep a mileage log. You can also ask your accountant about the pros and cons of the business owning the vehicle.

- **Make sure you're properly insured**

  Don't play games here — if you use your vehicle for business, tell your insurance company and make sure you are properly insured.

- **Don't talk on your cell phone while driving**

  I'm doing my part to make the world a better place. People who talk on cell phones while driving are idiots. Please don't be one of them.

- **Get that muffler fixed**

  I'm not telling you to go out and buy a new car, but make sure that if you're going to see clients that you don't arrive in an old beater that has bald tires, a leaking radiator, and no muffler. If your car needs repair, get it repaired (and trust me, the coat hanger thing *never* works). Your car should not be leaving big oil stains on your customer's driveway or parking lot (like mine once did … oops, that cost me a few bucks).

Chapter 31

COMPUTERS AND SOFTWARE

You are going to need a computer no matter what type of home-based business you wish to run. In this day and age, too much is done on computers for you to go ahead without one.

Even if you do no actual work on a computer and keep accounting records in a paper ledger, you will *still* need to use email to communicate with clients. I suppose you can get away without it, but more and more "old-timer" businesspeople (you know the type — grumpy, hardheaded, and often smelling of a decades old fragrance like Old Spice, Winston Cigarettes, or pot) are losing business to competitors who can communicate via email. I know I communicated with my last carpenter via email. It was pretty much a requirement for me.

I'm not going to spend a lot of time going over the computer itself and its individual parts (save for one). That's because the computer is becoming more and more like a TV — in all but the most extreme circumstances, almost any one you buy these days will do the job, and when it breaks, you will simply buy another one.

Just about any brand-name computer made in the last three years will run all common business software and will get online. There is almost no need to get into the "numbers" of gigahertz and bytes and such. I also don't recommend the cheapest model on the shelf — buy a midpriced one and you won't go wrong businesswise.

That being said, let's go over a few very important things regarding computers.

Learn about Them

I mentioned this earlier in the book, but hire a college kid or a neighbor's kid to teach you a few things about the computer if you don't know them. What follows are the things *I* think are most important:

- Windows Explorer (or similar) and file/folder structure. Learning "where" data is and how it is stored will help you immensely. Being able to create a new folder and learning how they are structured is a big step in understanding how things work on the computer. And you can learn it in maybe a half an hour.

- How to back up to another computer or a CD or DVD.

- Email and the Internet, including how to work with attachments. Learning how to FTP and how a website works won't hurt you either (but this last part may be a bit advanced — you may never really need to know this).

- How virus scan programs work.

- How to do basic things like write a letter or prepare an invoice.

Make Sure You Can Back Up Your Data

I've done tech support in the past, and I've been working with computers since the early '80s. Trust me when I tell you, the single most important aspect of computers is having all of your important data backed up on a regular basis. There is nothing more vital than that. So here's the only computer "part" I'll mention — a DVD burner (or whatever passes for a writable media in the future).

You will need a way to back up your data, and then it needs to be stored OFF-SITE. This way, if you have a fire, all of your computer and data files are safe. You can always buy another computer, pop in your disk, and there are your files.

Let me explain how I back up. Fair warning — I'm pretty nuts about this stuff. All of my work is done on computer, so I back up more than most people. Still, it takes almost no time.

First, I do a daily backup of several key folders to my laptop, which sits on another table. The computers are networked together. This way, if my main computer dies overnight, I'm right up to speed on the laptop.

Second, I burn a DVD every week of these same key folders. Since the DVD can hold massive amounts of data, I also back up personal stuff, such as pictures. I make sure my accounting files are password protected, in case someone else gets a hold of the DVD. I store these DVDs at a friend's house, and every month or so, I drop one in my safety deposit box as well (each backup is a "full" backup, meaning my friend only keeps the last four backups or so on hand — the rest I destroy). This means at worst, I'll lose a week's worth of data if I had a fire.

Third, any really important files that I wouldn't want to lose even a day's work on (like the manuscript for this book) get uploaded via FTP to a folder on my web host. Again, this may be a little advanced for some readers, but I'll also bet some of you out there are thinking, "Hey, that's a good idea — I never thought of that."

My backup routine has served me well. I've survived terrible, catastrophic crashes with no sweat at all. And I still have data that I wrote years ago, which has followed me from computer to computer to computer.

Keep the Kids Away from Your Work Computer

Kids can destroy computers. Especially young kids. They click on all sorts of weird things online, loading computers up with spyware, viruses, and more. And that purple dragon looked so innocent, too.

If possible, have a designated "kids computer" and an "adults only/business computer" if you are going to do any business-related computer work.

Get the Right Software

It's pretty hard to write a business proposal without a good word-processing program. Or to invoice without one. It's tough to keep your accounting records without the right accounting software either.

Good software makes your life easier. Some of it may come with your computer, but most good business programs don't (at best, a new computer may come with a trial version). Here's what I recommend:

- **An office suite**

  An office suite combines several popular business programs into one bundle: usually a word processor, a spreadsheet program, a publishing/graphic design program, and maybe an advanced email program. To be honest, many of you won't need an office suite. If all you're going to use the computer for is basic email, web surfing, writing an occasional letter and invoice, and accounting, you can likely do without one. However, if you are going to use the computer a lot in your business, and exchange files with clients, I recommend you get an office suite. It will make your life a lot easier. Though there are lower-cost (and free) alternatives, I use Microsoft Office Professional. Yes, it's a little pricey in terms of software, but I figured this is my business we're talking about, so I didn't mind spending the money. Other people may find that lower-cost or free software, such as OpenOffice, work just as well for their purposes.

- **An accounting program**

  Ask your accountant which brand to get. I use QuickBooks Professional.

- **Virus/spyware/firewall programs**

  Do yourself a big favor and spend a few bucks here: Buy a good, name-brand security program that does all three, and leave it at that. It'll likely update itself over the Internet, and you won't have to worry about these things (for the most part, so long as you follow some basic safety rules as well. In other words, don't click on that "click here" link that Meelo from Eastern Europe sent you out of the kindness of his heart). I like Trend Micro's PC-cillin.

All Kinds of Useful Programs You Never Knew Existed

Did you ever have a computer problem and remarked, "I wish someone made a program that …" Well, someone has probably made it, and it's probably available to download right now for about 20 to 50 bucks. Look around online — you'd be shocked at the amount of interesting and useful programs out there. I wanted a scheduling program, but had a specific way I wanted to do it. I found a program that keeps my schedule *exactly* like I want to. I found another program that organizes my notes. I found another that manages all of my passwords, and I found another that fully backs up Outlook Express (my email program).

I essentially typed what I was looking for the software to do into a search engine, and I found these programs.

Lastly, please pay for your software.

It never ceases to amaze me how many people think nothing of stealing software. Software is a tool. I use my word-processing program and office suite every single day. So what if it cost $400? Think about it — that's the main tool I use, and I've used it for several years now. Anyone who buys their own tools will tell you that's a bargain.

Not paying for your software is stealing. Period. If *you* want to be paid for *your* skills or product, you should be willing to pay others for theirs. Yes, even the big giant company deserves to be paid for its work.

Chapter 32

BUSINESS WRITING, LETTERS, AND SALES PROPOSALS

Business Writing

Let's face it — most people cannot write a good Christmas letter, never mind a winning business or sales letter. I'm going to try and change that to a small degree.

This isn't an indictment of people's writing skills in general. The problem is the way we are taught to write. We're taught to write "correctly," with complete sentences and well-thought-out paragraphs. We're taught to please the teacher, and avoid those horrid red marks on our papers ("see me after class" seemed to be a common one from my youth).

So as adults, we write timidly, making sure everything is correct — as if we were still writing for our sixth grade English teacher.

Know what? It's much better to write so people actually want to read what you write. Who cares if some of your sentences are fragments? Tons of mine are. In business, nobody is going to grade your paper. The pass/fail comes from your readers — if they read and understand what you wrote, you passed. If they are motivated to take action, you passed with flying colors.

But if you bored them, you failed. If they didn't finish your letter, you failed.

Listen, I'm a writer. I write for a living, and I wrote this book. And *I* don't pay much attention to the rules of proper English (not that I know very many). The rules are great to teach us when to use a period. But they tend to get in the way of good communication.

Good business writing (which is my specialty) would fail English class. It's really that simple.

But so what? I've written web copy that made website owners hundreds of thousands of dollars. Do you think those website owners cared if I used a fragment or three? Or used a ton of dashes? Or brackets (which, along with the dashes, I tend to use a lot of).

Okay, I'm getting off track here — let's get back to the business letter.

Business Letters

When most people write a business letter, they end up writing something like this:

> Dear Mr. Swanson,
>
> I'd like to take this opportunity to introduce myself and let you know of my company's services. My name is Lance Boil, and I run a vendor snacking service. I'm writing you today to offer my exclusive line of low-sodium, high-energy Pork Sticks …

Okay, let's stop — this is a terrible start to a letter. And not just because of the queasiness factor that Pork Sticks bring to mind (actually, if you think about it, strips of bacon are really Pork Sticks). However, most people won't even get to the benefits of the high energy pork sticks before they crumple up the letter.

That's because this letter DOES NOT ADDRESS THE READERS OR THEIR PROBLEMS. Instead, it says things like: **I'd** like to

take … introduce **MY**self … **MY** company … **MY** name … **I** run … **I'm** writing.

See a pattern? Me me me me me.

Almost all letters fall into this trap. It's how we are taught to write. We're taught to write in either first person (I), or third person (they) style. We almost never write in second person (you) style. However, second person is the most influential type of business writing. See, we're taught to write formal letters — introduce yourself, state what the letter is about, etc.

How about leading things off a little differently — which is interesting for readers — and perhaps even solving a problem for them? Yes, right in the beginning — don't lead off with the dry "I'd like to introduce …" but something the reader wasn't expecting.

Like this:

> Dear Mr. Swanson,
>
> How are your vending sales? Are they good? Or could they use a shot in the arm?
>
> How about your employees? Would they enjoy an exceptional new snack in your vending machines?
>
> What if your vending sales could increase, and at the same time, offer your employees an exciting, new, high-energy snack? Would that interest you?
>
> If so, read on.
>
> My name is Lance Boil, and I'm presenting you the opportunity to offer your employees the newest, most profitable snack item on the market today — Grandma Millie's Old Fashion Pork Sticks!

See the difference? This letter generally says the same thing as the first letter, except the first letter is much more formal, and "I" focused; the second letter is much more "you" focused. The second one is also far more exciting (well, as exciting as pork sticks can be), nontraditional, and bold. It also uses a one-sentence paragraph ("if so, read on") to great effect.

Assuming both letters were written in full in their respective styles, the second letter would likely outsell the first letter 50 to 1. But the first letter would likely get a better grade in English class. Which would you prefer?

Here are a few more writing tips:

- **Change it up**

  I led the letter off with an unconventional start. But you can go even further. Years ago, I'd send résumé cover letters that opened with, "I've had an interesting work history — would you believe that one time, I got fired for killing a rat?" …

  Then I'd introduce myself and why I was writing, and then quickly tell the brief (and true) story of how I was fired for being a rat killer. Would you believe that I got more calls from that cover letter than any "This letter is in response to your advertisement …" letter I ever wrote?

- **Short and sweet**

  Another thing that makes for effective business writing is to use short, punchy sentences and paragraphs. Make your writing easy to read.

Do you remember how you felt when you were in ninth or tenth grade, and the teacher gave you *Moby Dick* or *A Tale of Two Cities* to read? And your first thought as you looked at the 400-plus page tome was, "ugh … I have to read ALL THAT?"

Well, that's how your reader feels when presented with a 12-sentence paragraph. And since this isn't school, he or she is free to not read what you wrote and instead throw it away. There's no risk of staying after school. No bad marks. No vague threats of, "Mr. Furman, do you want to spend the rest of your life working in a car wash?"

Nope — your reader is an adult, and adults don't read things they don't want to read. Always remember that, and keep your writing short and punchy. And write like you're in the room, talking to someone.

- **Leave out the ten-dollar words**

  That's another thing — leave the corporate-speak out of your writing. Corporate people don't even talk to each other that way. (Most business-people don't know what the word *paradigm* really means, despite it being in every marketing document written since 1990.)

Listen, these tips aren't going to turn you into a professional as far as writing, but follow what I outlined and you'll become a MUCH better writer than you are now.

Never underestimate the power of a good letter. I recall the moment I decided to start my first business. In 1992, I had just finished a book by entrepreneur Harvey Mackay (he wrote *Swim with the Sharks Without Being Eaten Alive*, and has always been a source of inspiration to me). Anyway, I was so motivated by Harvey's book that I wrote him a nice letter telling him I was starting a business. Would you know that Harvey, who likely got 100 letters a day, not only wrote me back telling me what a great letter it was, but sent me a balloon bouquet congratulating me on my decision? (Too bad Harvey couldn't run my business for me — you've read all about the mistakes I made in this book.)

But the point is, my letter was good enough to make a millionaire CEO take notice! And if you read any of Harvey's stuff (highly recommended), you just *know* he didn't have some assistant write me — he did it himself. That little story has always been a source of motivation for me — a good enough letter can reach the top *anywhere*. Thanks, Harvey!

The Sales/Marketing Proposal

I charge people good money to write a two- to three-page sales proposal. I'm going to give you one for free. Check the CD for a sample.

My sales proposal is very similar to the "Pork Sticks" letter I began above. It's a quasi-letter that essentially introduces your company/service/product to a potential client, and attempts to sell them on it. It's bold, it's exciting, and it asks for the order.

My sales proposal starts off like a letter, but after a few paragraphs, it changes form a little bit — I might start using subheadings or bullet points. (Subheadings are bolded titles to a thought or paragraph — "The Sales/Marketing Proposal" that started off this section is a subheading.)

Subheadings and bullets draw the eye and satisfy people who scan instead of read. They also make your document *much* easier to understand.

It looks something like Sample 5 (a Word file that you can edit is on the CD).

Let's break it down into its components:

1. A one- or two-sentence beginning that focuses on the reader/and or their issues. Perhaps asks an important question.

2. Another one- to three-sentence paragraph. Useful to ask follow-up questions.

3. A two- to four-sentence "main point" paragraph. This alludes to the main point for writing. But still focuses more on benefits than actually getting into the entire reason for writing.

4. A one- or two-sentence "stinger" type paragraph (short, punchy, to the point), followed by a subheading or bullet points (or maybe both).

5. After these first four (which you don't have to follow exactly — this is just a guideline), mix it up with two- to four-sentence paragraphs, more subheadings, and more bullets. Keep it two to three pages (any more than that and it's probably too long).

A document like this can be useful for a lot of things — sales, getting an appointment, asking for money, etc. Just make sure you are conscious of the style I discussed in this chapter. Also, always ask yourself two things:

- What's in it for the reader?

- Is it easy to read?

Keeping those two simple things in mind as you write will dramatically improve any writing you do.

SALES AND MARKETING PROPOSAL

Joe Homeowner
226 Main Street
Anytown, NY 11111

3/21/2007

Dear Mr. Homeowner,

Is your home a candidate for an electrical fire?

Sorry, I don't mean to scare you, but honestly, have you ever considered what would happen if one of your home's electrical outlets were faulty, or had a loose wire, or had a switch that shorted out?

There are many different things that could go wrong with your home's electrical system — from a rodent chewing on a wire (more common than you think), to the coating on a wire dry-rotting away, to a loose outlet.

And these are things that don't become apparent until … well … you know.

That's the purpose of this letter — in short, we can help you prevent all this from happening.

Protecting Your Home from Electrical Fires

My name is Joe Electrician, owner of Joe's Electric, and we offer a service where we come into your home and do an inspection of your entire electrical system. If you ever wondered about the safety of your electrical system, this service is exactly what you need.

And this is a thorough inspection, too. Here's what we do:

- Inspect your panel and/or fuse box
- Check every outlet and switch for reliability and safety
- Check all visible wiring
- Inspect areas where rodents can get to wires and make sure there is no damage
- Check your household electrical current and identify short circuits and/or surges

Is Your Home Safe?

We've performed 78 inspections in the Anytown area in the last nine months. A full 70% of these homes had no problems at all.

However, that means 30% *did* have trouble. The trouble ranged from severely loose outlets that could short out, to several extremely dangerous situations where rodents had chewed into wires, to a faulty panel box.

In all cases so far, the homeowner *did not know* about the problems we found. It's very likely several fires were prevented.

Okay, how much does this service cost?

You're probably thinking, "How much?" To be honest, not many people from the "bad 30%" want us to walk away after finding a problem, so we do end up with the lion's share of the work.

For this reason, we offer this inspection service for what amounts to gas money — $50 for up to a 3,000 sq. ft. house.

Oh sure, you find problems and then fix them — gee, how convenient

I'd be lying if I didn't acknowledge that this service gets us business. However, we have a cut-and-dried policy — *we will NOT offer an estimate to fix anything unless <u>you</u> ask us to.*

In simple terms, you are free to use anyone you wish to fix any problems we find (or to not do anything about the problems at all). This service isn't so much about "getting us work" as it is "making people aware of their electrical problems."

We have an impeccable record with the Better Business Bureau, and are also long-term members of the local chamber of commerce. Our honesty and forthright business practices are second to none. Again, we will inspect your home, provide you with a detailed list of the electrical problems you have (if any), and then be on our way. If you want us to fix the problem, just ask, and we'll provide an estimate.

But you DO have to ask. Is that fair enough?

There's almost nothing worse than a house fire

Can you think of anything worse than a house fire in the middle of the night? Not much comes to mind, that's for sure. We can help prevent that from happening.

For $50.

To schedule your electrical safety inspection, just call us at (555) 555-1212 or visit our website at www.fakewebsitename.com.

I truly hope you will take advantage of this offer. These inspections have proven wildly popular, and our schedule fills up fast, so if you do want one, call today to set up an appointment.

Thank you for your time.

Joe Electrician, Owner
Joe's Electric

P.S.: Remember, nobody thinks about these things until after the fact. Don't let electrical mishaps happen to you.

Chapter 33

TRADITIONAL ADVERTISING AND YOUR HOME-BASED BUSINESS

This chapter is not meant to be a treatise on all the different forms of advertising — instead, it's meant to outline advertising for a beginning or small home-based business. That pretty much means no TV commercials in which you are the star. (More about that later.)

Advertising is very important to your business. Please do not think word of mouth is the way you're going to get all of your business. Maybe that works for Old Man McGeever who's been "plumbing this town since 1957," but it won't work for you.

Advertising is commonly misunderstood. It's the foolish business owner who looks at advertising as an expense. It's not an expense — it's an investment. Hey, I

spend over $500 per month advertising my home-based business. And one job — just one job — pays for it. The rest is gravy.

I'm not going to lie to you — advertising costs money. Sometimes a lot of money. A good-sized Yellow Pages ad will cost you hundreds of dollars. Online advertising (discussed in Chapter 36) can also cost hundreds. That's per month. But you must advertise if you want to succeed. Period.

In short, you will only get out of your business what you put into it. If you start your business and depend on homemade flyers hung on the supermarket bulletin board to get customers, well, expect no customers. Seriously, that's where Groovy Gary advertises guitar lessons and local teenagers advertise to cut lawns. A supermarket bulletin board is not the advertising medium you want to *depend on* for customers. Think about it: How many times have *you* hired a real business from one of those tear-off ads hanging on bulletin boards?

Fair Warning: When you first open your business, your local paper may report it in a small community interest segment — that nobody reads. Nobody except advertising salespeople, that is. Within a few weeks of starting your business, you may get swamped with salespeople contacting you to sell you advertising. And they all make huge promises about how many people will see your ad and how successful it will make you. For example, they'll say, "The cost per thousand makes this the best advertising value around," which essentially translates to "Hey, just buy some advertising, okay?" Advertising salespeople must have this subliminal ventriloquism thing down pat before they are let out into the wild, so keep your guard up, and instead listen to what I have to say here.

Newspapers

Three types of ads are run in newspapers: display ads, insert ads, and classified ads.

Display ads with pictures range in size from a few square inches to an entire page and are found throughout the paper. Depending on the circulation of your newspaper, running a display ad can be very expensive. Thus, commissioned advertising salespeople love to sell these ads.

Insert ads are, well, inserts that typically fall out of the paper. The Sunday paper is loaded with them. Again, these are likely very expensive; therefore, well-dressed, eternally cheerful advertising salespeople will happily sell you these, too.

Classified ads are your common "help wanted" or "autos for sale" ads. Ranging anywhere from three lines to a full column, these can be great buys. Since they are cheap, you typically have to call the paper yourself and speak to a disgruntled $7-per-hour employee to buy a classified ad.

Of the three types of ads, you will probably only be interested in classified advertising in the beginning. If your town or city has a small local paper, perhaps a display ad can be affordable, but other than that, I do not recommend spending your ad dollar for display ads until you get your feet under you. Classified ads make more fiscal sense when you are starting out.

In very simple terms, classified advertising can be extremely cost-effective, especially if you run an ad with any regularity (which you should). Most papers have a "local business" or "local services" section where you can run an ad for a very reasonable cost. People who read the classifieds and look at that section (and many people do) will see your ad all the time, which makes for a great, inexpensive way to get your name out there.

Classified ads are great for almost any type of business, whether you are offering a service or selling a product. See what headings your local paper has, and try to get in there. Many papers will offer a yearly deal — take it if you have the funds.

Tip: A catchy headline and using the word *you* in the ad is a great way to increase readership and the response rate of your ad. We are all human, meaning we are all selfish jerks — we LOVE it when something is about us. And in advertising, that translates to the word *you*. Take it from a professional business writer — *you* is THE most important word in business (forget "free"; "you" kicks its butt).

Radio

Radio ads are probably useless for most home-based businesses, at least in the beginning. Until you have plenty of money to spend on advertising, stay away from radio. I say you need plenty of money for one reason: *Radio only works when your commercial can play over and over, day after day, for weeks at a time*. That way, when someone is ready to make a buying decision, they say, "Lefty McNulty's Honest Accounting … I've heard of them."

Radio salespeople will tell you that radio can be excellent for building prestige. They'll mention that once you're on the radio, some clients will look at you like you've "arrived." Maybe that's true in some cases, but then why is the most expensive ad time always for the "morning zoo" type shows with names like "Jay Nutts and the Garbageman" or "Squeaky Wheels and the Greaser"? Yes, very prestigious indeed.

Still, once you have the funds and feel you are ready for the big time, radio can be a useful medium. It's often the first big advertising step a business takes when it makes the transition from the larval stage. For example, an accounting business (Lefty McNulty!) that moves from a home office to an outside office, or a contractor who is making the leap and putting a second crew

to work is probably ready for a six-month radio campaign.

> **BEWARE!**
>
> Radio salespeople often offer seemingly incredible deals. They'll tell you something like "Your commercial will run three times a day for four weeks, for only $--" (usually an astonishingly low rate).
>
> They do this because you'll likely say, "You mean I can be *on the radio* for *that*? Where do I sign up?"
>
> Never mind that your ad will run at 3 a.m. or some other odd time. And never mind that for these kinds of great deals they don't run your ad nearly often enough to be effective. They are simply counting on you not believing that you'll actually be on the radio for such a cheap price.
>
> Effective radio advertising is beyond the scope of most beginning home-based businesses. It's fine once you grow, but that's for another book.

Television

TV commercials are similar to radio in that they may be seen as prestigious indicators that you are a *real* business, and have arrived. They are also well beyond the budget of many start-up home-based businesses. Even the cheesy local commercials where the owner is the star are probably too expensive. Also, while I'm on that, do yourself a favor if you ever *do* have a TV commercial — stay out of it. Please? Or if you *must* be in it, don't yell and scream, okay? Really, is there anything more pathetic than a local "Car Wizard" or "Mattress King" doing his goofy schtick? If it were up to me (and sadly, it isn't), I'd disallow such self-made titles. In my world, you cannot be the Mattress King — you are merely a man who sells mattresses, no better than any other mattress peddler. I realize this is an unrealistic dream, and I'm getting away from my point, but it needed to be said.

Leaving cheesy commercials aside, there is one form of TV advertising that is often overlooked and can make a real difference for home-based businesses. Many local cable companies have a community channel where community events are posted. These channels often run ads for local businesses. Typically, these ads are just words on a blue background while long-forgotten '80s music plays and the local high school basketball scores scroll below.

Ads on such community events channels are usually dirt cheap, and they can be *very* effective for a home-based business. I have hired contractors from such ads. One job usually will pay for a year's worth of such ads, so this is worth investigating. Call your local cable company to see if they offer this service.

Yellow Pages

For any service-type business where your main market will be local, or if your business is the type where people might need you in an emergency, an ad in the Yellow Pages is an absolute must.

The following are some types of home-based businesses that will benefit from advertising in the Yellow Pages:

- Any building trades or contractors, including landscapers.

- Any home-based services such as daycare, hair styling, music lessons, etc.

- Any professional services such as accounting, surveying, computer networking, etc.

- Any other local services such as office or housecleaning, trash removal, home theater setup, etc.

In short, if you have any type of mainstream service that will serve the local market, *you must place an ad in the Yellow Pages*. If you're not in the Yellow Pages, you are not in business. It's really that simple.

The Yellow Pages companies know this, too — so the ads aren't cheap. A decent size ad will likely cost several hundred dollars a month. But then again, how much business does it pull? I know some hardheaded tradesmen who HATE all advertising, especially in the Yellow Pages — they simply hate spending $250 per month on an ad. Never mind that their phone rings four times a day due to the ad, and one job may pay for the ad tenfold. Never mind that they get almost ALL of their business from the ad. If you do the math (and sadly, most won't), Yellow Pages ads almost always pay for themselves. Believe me, they work, and they work well.

Look at the big picture here: If the ad is making your phone ring, it's almost always worth the money.

Now, you don't have to buy a big display ad right off the bat. You can buy an in-column "box" ad for a reasonable price. But here's the rule for the Yellow Pages: The bigger your ad, the more effective it is. This has been proven time and time again. Bigger *is* better.

Almost every Yellow Pages company usually offers superb deals to first-time advertisers. If you are in a business that will depend heavily on the Yellow Pages, take advantage of this — *buy the biggest ad you can realistically afford*. Yes, the price for your quarter-page ad will triple next year, but you can cross that bridge then. Either you will happily pay the increase (because it brings you business), or you will go to a smaller ad. But get the first year at the cheap rate.

Also, in most areas, there is more than one phone book. Which one should you be in? Well, all of them, if you can afford to. But if you cannot, pick the one that you (or your family) use most often.

Direct Mail

Direct mail can be a *very* effective form of advertising for a home-based business. There are several types of direct mail; which will be the most useful for you will depend on the type of business you have.

Before we even get into direct mail, I want to dispel the notion that direct mail is junk mail. Yes, I know full well that getting an advertisement for a new floral-scented thigh cream in the mail is probably not what you had in mind when you went to your mailbox. But you know, to someone else it's *exactly* what they are looking for.

There's an old saying in radio that every song, no matter how lousy, is someone's favorite song. This explains why "I Shot the Sheriff" gets airplay. Direct mail operates on a similar premise: There are people out there who will be interested in your product or service. It's simply a numbers game, and a matter of reaching them.

So direct mail tries to do this by blanketing "likely prospects" with your offer. Direct mail typically falls under three categories: 1) getting into local coupon packs or established "local savings" flyers; 2) sending mail to a targeted mailing list; or 3) sending mail to your own customer list.

Let's look at all three categories of direct mail.

Using local coupon packs/flyers

Pros — Inexpensive; superb local coverage; the ad company does almost all the work.

Cons — Not very effective if your business isn't local. Might be tough to get into due to exclusivity practices.

Using local coupon packs such as Money Mailer or Valpak coupons or the local flyers that come regularly in your mail is a great way to advertise in the local market. Usually, these packs are jam-packed with pizza coupons, video rental coupons, car wash coupons, "buy one get one free" coupons, etc. But they can be *great* for a home-based business as well.

Almost any type of local business can participate in coupon packs. True, they do lend themselves to "deals" like the above-mentioned buy-one-get-one-free (which does not work well for, say, a computer consultant). But almost any business can offer a "free consultation" or "10 percent off" to new clients. The point isn't so much your offer — it's being seen by potential clients. Direct-mail packs usually have a set number of local households they mail to — usually 10,000 per area. The ad companies do all the work for you — they'll likely even design your coupon/ad. All you have to do is provide the information. And the price is almost always pretty reasonable.

The really nice part is that many people look forward to getting these coupon packs. Being in the same envelope as that buy-one-get-one-free pizza coupon every month is almost like having a small store in the mall — JCPenney is the "anchor" store, and your store feeds off the traffic it generates. That pizza and/or video coupon that these packs always seem to have is the anchor.

Because they are valued and well known, these coupon packs overcome the usual "bulk mail curse" and actually get opened. I once made and sold my own direct-mail coupon packs, and as a lark, one month I inserted a coupon that had a funny story written on it. Would you believe that I got over 200 calls about the story? It meant to me that people were actually reading *all* of the coupons.

There are two drawbacks to these coupon packs: they aren't very good if your business isn't local, and some of them practice exclusivity. Exclusivity means only *one* pizza place gets in, and only one exterminator, one painter, one plumber, etc. You'll have to ask your salesperson about this. Rate of return for direct-mail packs like this vary, but a 1 percent return would be phenomenal for an ad that did not offer "buy one get one free."

HINT: Start saving your junk mail. Take a good look and see what businesses are included, and what they are advertising (this is also how you contact the company doing the mailer). There is no better way to gauge an effective ad pack than by seeing the same businesses in them over and over.

Using targeted mailing lists

Pros — Highly targeted.

Cons — You usually have to do much of the labor yourself. It can be a lot of work if you have hundreds of pieces to send out.

Targeted mailing lists are usually used when you have a niche business or one that covers a very wide geographical area (statewide or nationwide). Let's say you offer a web design service. Perhaps you want to target marketing managers of mid-size corporations. So you buy a mailing list of just those people (oodles of companies sell lists; just search online for "direct mail lists" for a specific town), and send them a nice sales letter. Or perhaps you have a gadget or service that you want to sell to auto parts stores. So you buy a list of auto parts stores, and you produce a postcard showing your gadget or detailing your service, and you mail it out to them.

This can be very effective because it is targeted. However, you usually have to do a lot of the legwork here. You have to make the list, you have to make (or design) the postcard/letter/whatever it is you want to send, and you have to stuff the envelopes. (Granted, you can pay someone to do all of these things, but for home-based businesses, this usually isn't cost-effective.)

Acceptable rates of return vary, but 2 to 3 percent is usually considered very good. This means out of 100 pieces sent, two to three will call you. This doesn't seem like much, but consider how much one client is worth (more on advertising returns a bit later).

By the way, when sending out your own direct mail, never *ever* use bulk-rate postage. Use a real first-class stamp.

Using your own mailing list

Pros — Super targeted to people who know you and have done business with you.

Cons — You have to do most of the work.

Rather than buying an outside list, you can use your *own* mailing list compiled from former clients/customers (you do have a list, right?).

Sending your customer list a postcard/letter detailing your latest sale, latest specials, or just a reminder of your services can be a gold mine. That's because these are people who have already used your service.

Think of it like dating — these are customers you already took out and had a good time with. There is no awkward getting-to-know-you phase, no having to meet their parents, none of that. You are already familiar with each other, so you can go right to the good stuff.

Again, rate of return varies, but all things being equal, you should generally expect double the rate of return you would get using an outside list.

Specialty Advertising

Specialty advertising is a fancy name for doodads and gizmos with your name on them. A pen with your business name on it. A mug with a clever saying. T-shirts for your employees. And so on.

For a home-based business, these gadgets are great for two things:

1. Wasting your money.

2. Giving you a tangible memento of the brief time you ran a business, because a new business that spends money on this crap won't be around very long.

I don't mean to be harsh, but let's just say I still have a 15-year-old Intriguing Ideas jacket hanging in my closet. This jacket is a sad reminder that I was once foolish enough to waste several hundred dollars on six of these — at a time when paying the rent was difficult. (It's also a reminder that I used to wear a medium, a size I have not seen in quite some time.)

Save your money for now. The imprinted jackets and shirts and pens are nice "prestige" items, and can indeed be nice gifts to clients. And yes, they will make you feel good wearing them and giving them out. I'm not saying you should not indulge in this type of thing, but wait until you can truly afford it. It's all the sweeter then.

There is one exception to this rule for a start-up business — for many trade businesses (carpenter, handyman, etc.), a business card magnet is a very wise investment.

What to Say in an Ad

As a writer, I could write an entire book on this topic. So in the interest of brevity and not boring you with things that don't pertain to your business, I'm going to go over the finer points of writing that everyone needs to know.

People trip on what to write in an ad all the time. They never know quite what to say, so they end up saying *way* too much. People are afraid of white space in an ad. If they see unused space, they cram it with something. Usually a silly, meaningless slogan.

There's a simple rule to remember when writing an ad for most home-based businesses: *An ad's goal is to make your phone ring.*

That's it — that's your goal.

The ad isn't there to close the deal or to sing the praises of every single thing you do — it's meant to make a customer say, "This is someone I should call." Write your ads with that in mind. Save the entire sales pitch for when you are talking to your client.

I mention this because too many business owners feel they need to say everything in an ad. It almost seems as if they expect the ad to make the sale. It won't, so don't even try. Like the revised business card shown in Chapter 28, say enough to get a phone call, and that's it.

So how do you do this? Remember two things:

1. Write down the five most important things you can get across to your potential clients. Use these as the core of your ad. You don't need to get across all five, but this gives you a good start on what's important.

2. Remember that almost everyone who reads your advertisements has a problem, and your ad needs to solve their problem. For example, if you have an in-home daycare, your potential client has a childcare problem. SOLVE THAT PROBLEM. So a small Yellow Pages ad might not be the place to discuss the lunch menu.

Also, as I mentioned earlier, omit silly slogans like "One Call, That's All" or "Knowledgeable and Reliable" from your ad. They aren't witty, clever, or meaningful in any way — all they do is clutter your ad and make it a jumble of words. Do you really think a customer reads the ad and says, *"Oh look — they're knowledgeable AND reliable, a combination you don't often see these days. Let's call!"*

On that note, it probably doesn't help much to put "friendly service" in an ad either. As opposed to what? Surly service? Disinterested service?

Why *would* a business have to say they have "friendly service" in an ad? Isn't that … kind of just expected? I'm not opposed to putting something like that on your website's "about us" page or on some longer form of marketing, but in a small advertisement? Not needed, and wasteful.

What to Expect from Your Advertising

It's very important for you to have realistic expectations for your advertising results. I say this with a grain of salt, because I used to sell advertising. And let's just say I heard a lot of "no thank-yous" (and it sounded an awful lot like "get the @#$% out of my face" to me, but that's just semantics).

My point is, many businesspeople do not understand advertising. Let's take a direct-mail pack — say a computer consultant/repair business gets into a direct-mail pack, pays $500 to be in it, and it goes out to 10,000 people. The campaign generates 14 phone calls (a fairly low rate of return, but perhaps expected for a computer business, which isn't a traditional "coupon pack" business). Out of those 14 phone calls, ten were just people fishing, looking for a deal, etc. But four turned into jobs, and two of those four jobs turned into commercial clients.

Success or failure?

Most business owners would say "failure." The advertising only generated 14 phone calls out of 10,000 impressions, and only resulted in four jobs. Harrumph — $500 down the drain.

I, however, would call it a stunning success. For a business such as computer consulting/repair, four jobs and two new commercial clients that will likely provide *years* of invoicing is well worth a $500 investment. Plus, there is the added benefit of referrals those two clients will generate (say they each generate one referral a year, and each referral generates one, and so on).

That coupon pack will likely pay for itself again and again and again.

That's how you have to look at advertising.

Track your ads. Know who's calling. Watch how they work, and look at the big picture.

It sounds simple, but so many people only look at the raw dollars of how much an ad costs. And they compare that dollar figure to phone calls and direct responses.

Don't do that.

When I sold ads for Yellow Pages, I recall one contractor whose Yellow Pages ad made the phone ring fairly consistently (it got him maybe five calls a week, which for him equaled a new job every other week, as he generally got one job for every ten callers). Not only did these calls provide thousands and thousands of dollars in direct jobs, but they produced satisfied clients who would all too happily provide referrals. It's a snowball effect, really.

But this contractor, being ignorant about advertising in general, canceled his ad. Why? Because he felt the $250 a month wasn't worth it. For starters, he HATED that he got only one client out of ten calls. He HATED the people who were just fishing, looking for a price, etc. So he saw his ad as an annoyance generator (*"Nine out of ten calls are useless price shoppers!"* he said).

He also could not see beyond, "Why should I pay $250 a month to be in the phone book when I can put an ad on the supermarket bulletin board for free?" (That's exactly what he said to me.) Try as I might, I could not convince him otherwise. He simply did not care how much business the ad got him. All he cared about was that it cost $250 a month, and nine out of ten callers were "idiot price shoppers."

Guess what happened to him? He was out of business within two years — partly because of his attitude toward advertising.

This isn't to say you have to buy every ad that a salesman solicits. But you have to look at your advertising beyond just "cost" or "number of responses," and instead look at how much *business* an ad actually brings you, both in the short term and the long term. Test the waters and jump in when you feel the temperature is good.

Chapter 34

THE INTERNET AND YOUR WEBSITE

The Internet is easily the biggest thing to happen to home-based businesses since … well … since ever, really. Think about what is possible with the Internet:

- From your home, you can easily offer your services to the entire world.

- Not only can you offer your services to everyone, you can offer them to people particularly searching for your specialty.

- For any business (local or international), you can have a website that acts as a salesperson, on call 24 hours a day, seven days a week. Your website can give so much more information than a simple business

card or brochure can. And the cost for this? It's dirt cheap.

Years ago, someone like me (a "good writer" without any real credentials) had almost no hope of selling my service to the world. Since I had no college degree, the best I could do was perhaps join an ad agency. But even then, there was a slim chance of getting in, and I'd have to move to where the agencies were. Oh sure, people had been telling me for 20 years, "You're a good writer — you should get into that." Well, how? It just seemed there was very little need for a business writer like me.

Actually, I was wrong — there *was* a need. But there was no practical way for me to reach this market.

Until the Internet came along.

Now, people all over the world can search for a "business writer" or a "professional writer" and *bam* — there's my ad. They click my ad, and they go to my website (this is called pay-per-click advertising, which I'll get into in depth in Chapter 36). Now, they can read my website (which is written by me, in my style), decide if they like my writing, and click to email me.

It's so simple, it's almost astonishing. I literally do business with people all over the world. Anyone who needs writing can easily find me.

It's been said that if you can't find it on the Internet, then you have found a need (which you might want to work on filling). You can find just about *anything* on the Internet. I'll never forget the first day I went online all those years ago. (I've been on the Internet since before Al Gore invented it.) My first search was … well, you can probably guess what I searched for — I was in my early twenties and single. But I found it (and how!).

Okay, enough on the introduction to the Internet. Let's discuss exactly how the Internet can help your home-based business.

Why You Need a Website

Obviously, if you have a business like mine, or do any work beyond your local area, you will need a website. So I'm going to skip those obvious examples and instead talk to the local businesses that think they don't need one.

Reason one — people expect it

In this day and age, people simply expect you to have a website. Any business without a website is looked at negatively by a growing segment of the population. I even want my drywall guy to have a website, so I can at least find his email address.

So I don't care who you are or what your business is, you need a website — if only to satisfy a guy like me (who is part of your customer base). I hired my last carpenter off the Internet. And the tree pruner I found in the Yellow Pages, but I checked his website to see a picture of his bucket truck (I wanted a guy with a bucket truck, not a climber).

Reason two — image

A website simply means that you are in business. These days, anyone *without* a website isn't truly in business (in my opinion). Having a www name and a "real" .com email address is what separates *real* home-based businesses from scrapbooking services.

Reason three — marketing

A professional, well-written website is like a supersalesperson. On call, 24 hours a day, seven days a week. You can have samples of your work, customer testimonials, why someone should do business with you, helpful hints, before and after pictures, etc.

A local business with a nice website is light years — really, light years — ahead of the competition. For example, a roofer, a DJ, or an accountant with a nice website (and who knows how to use it) can very quickly rise above his or her competition.

YOU DON'T NEED TO START WITH ANYTHING ELABORATE

Now, you may not need a large, professionally designed website at first. But I recommend *every* home-based business have at *least* one page with the following information:

- Business name

- What you do

- How to contact you (with an email link)

You may not need any more than that, for now. But that single, solitary page puts you WAY out in front of your competition. It also gives you the benefit of being seen as a *real* business.

Here's How You Get a Website

1. Decide on a domain name. This is going to be your www address. Now, I must warn you, all of the good generic ones are taken. However, get creative here. As I mentioned in Chapter 3, at the time of this writing, Bob the Florida exterminator can get www.ikillfloridabugs.com. Your website name need not be your business name. My business name is technically Night Owl e-Ventures Inc. My main website is www.clear-writing.com. Most people think my business name is "clear writing." It matters not to me.

   Now, an aside here: You can have as many domain names as you want. I have both clear-writing.com and nightowleventures.com pointing to one website. If you *can* get your business name as a domain name, I suggest you lock it up, even if you'd rather use a "clever" one. The reason to lock up the one for your company name is that if an angry customer found out your company name domain name was free, this customer — or anyone else — could buy it and put up a porn site. For the scant amount of money it costs, it makes sense to lock up your company name if it's available (and it may not be).

2. After you decide on a domain name (or several), go to www.godaddy.com or www.register.com to "register" your name. There you can search to see if your name is available (you'll get results right away). You may have to keep trying until one you want is free.

3. Once you get one that's open, follow the directions and register it. It costs only a few bucks a year. That's it. You now have a domain name.

4. Now you need "hosting" — space where your website will go. You can buy hosting from the company you bought your domain name from (both those I mentioned offer hosting, and I personally have used both to great satisfaction). You may want to research a few of the hosting options available. When you get hosting, make sure it comes with a few email accounts. Almost all do. Now

you'll have a business email of your name@yourwebsitename.com, which is very professional and desirable.

5. Okay, you have your domain name, and you have your hosting. Building your website and getting it online could easily fill the rest of this book, so this is one of those instances where you're going to have to either do some reading and/or find someone to help you. (Most hosting sites have a fairly easy-to-use "site builder," although I recommend you only use these to get your feet wet, as the sites they produce look amateur.) The information is out there, it's very easy to understand, and you *can* do it. And trust me, once you get that first page up, and you make a change to it, then get your changed page up … well, it gets *very* addicting.

Working from Home, *At* Home

I have to admit, I am very hyped about the Internet as a serious business tool for those who want to work from home, *at* home. As you already know, that's what I do. I can offer my services to anyone, anywhere. To this end, I've put up an extensive website that (hopefully) tells people I'm the guy they should be doing business with.

My business is writing. Yours may be marketing, data entry, accounting, résumé writing, life coaching, medical billing … whatever. For example, do you know how many lawyers use outside transcribing services? A *ton*. With the Internet, if you have a transcribing service, lawyers send you the recorded files via email, you transcribe them, and you send them back by email.

There is no need for both of you to be in the same town, never mind the same time zone — distance just isn't a factor anymore. Do you realize just how exciting this is?

Take the above scenario and apply it to *any* desk job. Through virtual meetings and remote access tools, it is possible to do virtually any desk job from your home. But I'm not talking about finding a company that will let you work from home. They are few and far between. Much more prevalent are companies that simply farm out these tasks to consultants/freelancers … in other words, HOME-BASED BUSINESS OWNERS.

I recently wrote the website text for a woman who owns her own data entry business. Essentially, companies hire her when they have massive amounts of data to enter into computers. It makes sense for a company to hire her — they pay no benefits, the work gets done, and when the project is finished, they both move on. So how many companies need this sort of thing? I'll bet the number is somewhere in the tens of thousands. Probably more than need a writer (maybe I'm in the wrong business?).

All of this is possible because of the Internet.

Scams

In this chapter, I'm talking about practical uses of the Internet for a real home-based business. I am not talking about the seemingly endless supply of online scams that make it seem like you can just set up a website and let the cash roll in.

Listen, there is no easy money. For every person that caught lightning in a bottle and had a great idea that made millions on the

Internet, there are thousands and thousands of people who came to the party late and bought some "system" that promised endless wealth doing the same thing … but the wealth in question goes to the seller of the system.

Stay far away from those long web pages with red headlines, shocking testimonials, yellow highlights, and today's date on the top (that's really a trick — it's a piece of code that automatically puts in today's date). Also be wary of anything that starts off with "Dear Friend." Trust me, they aren't your friend. They should say, "Dear Sucker," because that's what they are really thinking, but test marketing proved that "Dear Sucker" turned people off. "Dear Loser" and "Dear Schmuck" didn't test much better, so they eventually settled on "Dear Friend," which sounds a little warmer. But trust me, "Dear Friend" is another way of saying, "I'm going to play with your emotions and make you feel like you will miss the boat if you don't order *right now*."

I even found one of these pages geared toward writing. The site was *so* over the top, *so* outrageous, that it made me spit out my coffee in laughter. It said something like this:

> Become a copywriter and work as much or as little as you want!! Work from the mountains, the beach, or anywhere!! Write while listening to gentle ocean waves!! Why, I wrote all last summer from a 16th-century Spanish villa while perfumed servants threw fresh flowers at my feet as I walked to the fountains bubbling with pure vintage wine!! Then a nine-course meal was prepared, and once the prime minister finished waxing my Jaguar …

Okay, obviously I'm exaggerating, but it may as well have said so (to be honest, I'm not even sure if Spain *has* a prime minister). The point is, the website's author implied that you too could get that lifestyle, if you just buy his book!

Well, I have to tell you, being a writer really isn't like that. Oh, it has its moments, but I can't work "as little as I want" (which would roughly translate to "not at all"). And true, I can technically work from the mountains if I wish, but I kind of have to be able to *afford* a mountain place. My writing pays well, but it doesn't pay *that* well. Maybe Stephen King can afford that lifestyle, but not me.

I'm also leaving out the obvious point that you aren't learning how to be a million-dollar writer from a book. No matter what Dave from California (him again, huh?) says.

There is no easy money. There is no get rich quick. The Internet is extremely useful to help your real business succeed. But steer clear of the scams.

One Last Thing — Website Conversion

Website conversion is simply the number of visitors coming to your website versus the number of "actions" (emails, phone calls, orders) your website generates. See, just getting people to look at your website isn't enough. Your site has to convince them to contact you. This is not an easy thing to do

— there are literally millions of homemade websites on the Internet that do a terrible job of converting visitors into contacts. Such sites are usually made by people who say the Internet "doesn't work." Well, of course the Internet isn't going to work if you try to convince me with text like this:

> Plump Turnip Contracting has been in business since 1998 and has won numerous awards for our quality work. We are a leader in quality building in the Anytown area. We have the lowest prices and the best service so why not go and save yourself some money and give us a call.

This was from an actual site (well, I changed the name). It's not terrible, but it's boring as heck, and it doesn't address the reader's issues at all. You're not convincing anyone to click through with wording like that.

There are scores of books written on the subject of the Internet and website conversion. I suggest you get one of them if you are going to use your website to drive business to you.

You must have a clear, compelling message, and it must be persuasive. Otherwise, nobody will contact you.

Chapter 35

EMAIL (IT'S MORE IMPORTANT THAN YOU THINK)

Email is no longer a niche communication device — it is now fully mainstream.

To give you an idea of how far email has come, consider the fact that in some cases, I have done thousands of dollars of business for people and for companies that I have never spoken a word to. And I'm not talking about big, impersonal projects. I worked directly (and extensively) with individual people, and we communicated back and forth hundreds of times — all via email. In fact, at this writing, I have yet to actually "speak" to my publisher for this book. Oh, we've communicated quite a bit, asking and answering questions, sending contracts back and forth to be signed, etc. But we don't know what each other's voices sound like. Do you find that odd? I don't. To

me (and a growing segment of the population), it's normal.

All because of email.

You are going to need to use email, no matter what your business is. I don't care if you're the ultimate "nontechnological" carpenter who's been successful for 30 years — you will lose business if you don't use email. Today's clients almost demand it. In fact, I won't hire someone I can't email. It's easily my preferred method of communication.

There are several reasons why email has become so popular:

- **Email is very convenient, and saves time**

I'd rather email than talk on the phone. In fact, the phone is almost impractical. To use the phone, we both have to be free at the same time. Not so with email. I send you a message, you get back to me when you are able, I send you another, etc. We can have an entire conversation and never be awake at the same time.

- **Email is very fast, and you can attach files**

I can send an email across the world in seconds. I even invoice my clients via email. Instead of sending a paper invoice through the mail (and having it take days to get there), I can attach an invoice to an email and send it to my client. This way, I get paid faster, and the email goes right to the desk of the person who pays it. I can also send my clients large documents/files (and vice versa) in seconds.

- **You can truly multitask with email**

I can get email while working, and it's no bother. I can get four emails at once, and it's no problem. And nobody ever gets a busy signal.

Now I'm not saying that email totally replaces the phone or letters — it doesn't. But it has grown to become a vital part of business. I would say email is *at least* as important as the phone. Probably more so. If I could choose only one communication method to use for business, I would choose email.

- **You will lose business if you don't use email**

It's a big advantage for your business if you are not only comfortable with email, but proficient in using it. If you work in an office, email is probably a very big part of your job, but I personally know plenty of local service people who cannot/will not use email.

I gotta tell you — they are losing business. People like me want to communicate via email, and I'm not hiring you to do my roof if I'm reduced to playing phone tag with you.

Email Marketing

Email is an incredible marketing/sales tool because you can easily keep in touch with clients and send them something like a monthly newsletter at no cost. In fact, you can send a newsletter to your entire mailing list with a simple click. *That's* power (and now we see why spam is so prevalent).

The simplest, most overlooked business generator I know of is keeping in touch with your clients, both present and past. It keeps your name in front of them, and always reminds them that you are there, just a click away. Sending your client email list an occasional, informative newsletter is the best way to spur business.

I don't care what type of home-based business you own: Get your client's email addresses when they first start doing business with you, and send them something every so often. Make it interesting and related to your business. If you have a computer repair business, send a "free computer tips" sheet every other month teaching people how to defrag and other useful skills. If you're a DJ, send a newsletter with the top 100 party songs every few months. If you're an electrician, send a newsletter every other month teaching a basic electrical safety tip. (Don't worry, you're not going to create an army of electricians to compete with you, nor will anyone really use your tips instead of calling you. I have free writing tips on my website — it hasn't hurt business one bit.)

Yes, most people will simply delete your email. But some will read it. And of that some, a few may need (or know someone who needs) your service. *There's no downside to doing this — only an upside.*

Keep in mind, if you do send regular newsletters (and most of you won't, but for the few who actually said "hmmm, sounds like a neat idea, Dan"), make sure to let your customers know they can opt out of any future emails at any time (we don't want to be pests now, do we?).

Have I convinced you yet? Have I convinced you that email is vital? Good. Let's move on to my email rules.

Dan's Email Rules

1. Get a real email address

If you are going to be in business, you won't go wrong getting a professional email address. It simply conveys an image of professionalism and competence. I have to admit, I hesitate when I'm doing business with someone who has an obvious "home" email address, especially if I'm writing to a handle such as "bigandsexy." So I recommend you use a regular business email address with simply your name.

I mentioned in Chapter 34 that you should get a domain name, which becomes your business email as well. Almost all hosting includes email accounts, and usually has instructions on how to set them up.

Thus, you become john@your domain.com (assuming your name is John, of course), which is a lot better than john45933@someisp .net. And as I already stated, let's keep the business email address businesslike. Unless you're in the porn industry, "studmuffin69" is probably a bad email address to choose. You can always create second or third email addresses that you give to family and friends, so your prized "cuddlygrrrlll" handle can still exist. But for business, simply your first name at your domain will do nicely.

2. Answer your email

Unless you are on vacation, you should answer your email every business day. Three times a day, really — once in the morning, once in the afternoon, and once in the evening. And every client who emails you deserves a reply (unless none is expected). Email is a "now" communication — do not keep people waiting.

I get comments from clients all the time about how prompt I am at answering email. It's a really simple way to stand out.

3. Keep your email neat

Forget signatures such as "this information is confidential" or "the contents have been virus scanned" on your emails. They are annoying, and essentially scream "stuffy corporate weenie." They also really get in the way when an email gets replied to several times — do we really need to see this ten-line signature eight times?

A signature with your name, title, website address, and maybe your phone number is fine. But keep the "corporate speak" out of it (or even worse, Monty Python and the Holy Grail quotes or whatnot). Listen, I like the Holy Grail as much as the next guy (probably more), but not everyone in the business world is amused by the exploits of Sir Lancelot the Brave; Sir Galahad the Pure; and Sir Robin the not-quite-so-brave-as-Sir Lancelot.

In addition, plain text email is the way to go. Forget background images, pictures, etc. These types of emails often get flagged as spam.

4. Forget the spam filters for your incoming mail

I know, I know — spam is a problem. I get nine messages a day offering me "the lowest prices on pharmaceuticals." I assume they want me doped up so I'll respond to one of the seven messages asking me to remortgage my house "at unheard of rates." Spam is even starting to get personal, insinuating that perhaps Maryellen isn't as ... well

... satisfied as she could be with me (and of course, this email promises to fix that). How they got this information, I don't know — I would hope that if Maryellen were unhappy with me in any way, she'd tell me, and not confide in some anonymous email company in Eastern Europe. Unless, of course, that's where she's been going because she's unsatisfied ...

Anyway, yes, spam is a problem. But a bigger problem is the spam filters many people use. Let me explain why.

Spam filters are software. Software, good as it may be, can never truly 100 percent tell spam from real business email. If it is successful 99 percent of the time, that means 1 percent of the time it fails. That means 1 out of 100 business messages is lost. Now, that may not seem like a big deal, but consider 100 business messages is about three days' worth for me. I do *not* want to lose one legitimate email every three days. What if one was a quote request for a six-month, six-figure project? And if I don't reply, well, they'll figure I wasn't interested. Would you like *that* to be the one email your spam filter catches? I wouldn't.

And don't think that can't happen. I have done *huge* projects for people, projects that have made my entire year — and they all started with one email. Had I missed that first email, well, nothing would have happened. Had I missed the email from Richard telling me he wanted to publish this book, he likely would have thought I wasn't interested and moved on.

In short, you cannot afford to miss even *one* important email.

In addition, think about this logically: You are asking a program to sort your email. Would you ask your human mail carrier to do that? Would you go up to your mail carrier and say, "Hey there *[insert your mail carrier's name]*, would you mind sorting through my mail before you deliver it to me, and throw away anything you think is junk mail?"

Of course you wouldn't do this. So why would you ask the exact same thing from a piece of software? You shouldn't.

On the other side of the coin are those spam filters or services that ask senders to "register," so they won't flag me as spam in the future. Know what I do? I ignore them, and don't do business with these people.

Don't put up roadblocks to business because you don't want to see a little spam. Use your delete key and delete the spam — it takes about ten seconds a day. It also makes for interesting reading when one is bored.

5. **Never send email when you are angry**

Never, ever, ever, ever, ever. If you must write an angry email, go ahead and write it, and save it, but don't send it. Then read it when you aren't so angry and see if you still want to say the same things. I'll bet you don't.

6. **Don't be afraid of using attachments**

I send/receive probably 20 attachments a week. No, I don't open obvious "click here for a big surprise" attachments, but my business is such that I must use attachments. Don't be afraid to use them. If you have good virus software and keep your files backed up (in case your virus software fails), you won't have anything to worry about.

Chapter 36

INTERNET ADVERTISING — SEARCH ENGINES, PAY-PER-CLICK, PRESS RELEASES, AND OTHER THINGS YOU MAY NOT KNOW ABOUT

While the Internet is a great way to advertise, it's sometimes misunderstood. That's because almost all Internet advertising is really not meant to advertise *your business* per se — it's meant to advertise your website. Then your website does the job of advertising your business — it's a two-step process.

The only situation where the Internet is used to advertise your business is in a paid listing, which I'll discuss. But every other aspect of Internet advertising is website based.

Okay, here's Internet advertising in a nutshell.

Paid or Free Directory Listings

There is no central "Internet listing service." All Internet "listings" are really just websites that list business names. For example, on a local level, your Chamber of Commerce or business association may have free or paid Internet listings for your area. This means that when someone searches for a contractor in Anytown, USA, your listing might come up if you're a contractor in that area. Yellow Pages companies are also starting to offer paid listings on their websites, which work in the same way.

I want to caution you about these listings. They are great for getting your name

135

in front of Internet searchers; however, they are ineffective if you don't *also* have a website. *Don't think they are a replacement for a website in any way.* Here's why: Along with the listing comes a link to your company website — *if you have one.* People searching for a business online will not just find you; they will also find your competition. Since they are already online, 99 percent will not write down phone numbers — they will simply choose contractors that have website links, and go to them.

Listings are great if you have a website. They are a very effective marketing tool, particularly at the local level. But if you don't have a website, you will likely see very few results from your online listing. Still, it's probably better than not being online at all.

The following discussion about Internet advertising will only be relevant if you have a website.

Search Engine Ranking

People use search engines and directory services such as Google and Yahoo! to find what they are looking for online. Type in "business writer" and millions of websites come up. There is a very competitive, cut-throat scramble to get to the top of these rankings. Companies specialize in tweaking your website so it gets higher and higher on search engine listings.

I'm not going to explain this topic in depth — partly because the search engines keep tweaking the rules, so anything I tell you here could be invalid by the time you read this book. I do suggest that if you are interested in optimizing your website, you read up on search engine optimization and key words (also spelled as one word). You

can go online or buy a book dedicated to this topic.

However, there are a few pieces of advice I *can* give you that will help your website's rankings:

- Make sure your website provides *useful, informative* information on the topic it covers. For example, if you are a carpenter, have a page for each specialty you do, plus a few pages of basic carpentry tips.

- Update your website often. Usually adding a monthly article will be enough. At this writing, blogs are popular as well. If you want to invest the time, a blog can be an effective way to communicate your expertise to your website audience. (When I say blog, I do NOT mean a personal blog. Trust me, nobody cares what songs you are listening to or your opinions on government.)

- Try to get legitimate links on other websites that go to your site. For example, if any of your clients have websites, ask them to link to your site. I say "legitimate" because there are "link farms" out there that promise you lots of links back to your site for a fee. Don't subscribe to them. They could get you banned from search engines. Keep your links legitimate.

- Participate on web forums and newsgroups related to your industry, and put your website link in your signature. This can be a very effective tactic, as your postings can show up in search engines. Plus, it's almost always free. To find forums for your industry, just go to any search engine and type in *"your industry* discussion forum."* Find a forum that looks interesting, register, and start reading the messages. When you feel you can add something, do so (see Chapter 49 for more on online forums).

- Create highly targeted, legitimate links back to your site in the form of press releases (see the following section).

Press Releases

Press releases are simply news bulletins about your business. Many news publications look to newswires to get stories. This is where press releases come in. We're going to skip traditional distribution of press releases, and instead focus on their distribution online.

Online, a press release does two things: It's a nice little story about your business, and it creates a link back to your website. In fact, sometimes it can create thousands of links. If your story is interesting enough, it might be picked up by hundreds or thousands of online publications, all having links back to your site. Sweet.

And here's the best part — they're free. That's right — you can write and release a press release for free — every day if you care to. How do you do this? Go to www.prweb.com and sign up. Once there, you can learn how to write a press release (it's easy — and to help you, I have included a sample on the CD) and how to "release" it. Releasing it is as easy as sending an email — it's free and you do it right on prweb.com. You can also pay to get your press release to reach more news outlets, but you need not partake if you don't want to.

In addition, you should consider emailing a link to your release to your local newspaper (hey, maybe they'll pick it up).

Press releases are a fantastic source of advertising, and nobody uses them. Everybody should — every single business should do at least one a month. *Anything* can be news. You can write a release stating "Local daycare uses Internet technology to satisfy consumer demand," which means you answer clients' email. Almost anything you can think of can be made newsworthy. I can make the fact that you found pocket lint this morning into a news story.

Pay-per-Click

There's another reason I told you not to bother much with natural search engine rankings right now, and it's called "pay-per-click." Pay-per-click is just what it sounds like — you pay when someone clicks on your ad. It's a wonderful way to advertise.

In a nutshell, pay-per-click allows you to "buy" key words or phrases. When the key word or phrase is typed into the search engine, your ad comes up (along with others from businesses that bought the same key word). When someone clicks on your ad, you pay a certain amount — perhaps 50 cents.

What this means is, your ad will *only* appear to people searching for what you do. My ad appears to people searching for business writers (among other things). My little ad tells them what I do (I'll admit there's some competition to have a good ad that people will click on), so the people clicking are already *very* interested in my services. I'll happily pay for that.

Are you beginning to see how powerful pay-per-click is? It gets better. If your business serves only local clients, you can choose that your ad only appears in certain geographical areas. Or your ad can include your town as a key word, so that people searching Google for a local plumber/roofer/daycare/photographer/DJ (and many are these days) can find your ad. And it's *very* likely many of your competitors are not aware of this.

You can go to www.google.com or www.overture.com for more information.

These are all the Internet advertising vehicles I'm going to discuss. There are a few more flavor-of-the-months, but the ones I've covered in this chapter should be plenty for your home-based business to sink its teeth into.

Chapter 37

PERILS OF THE 80/20 RULE

It's been said that 80 percent of your business will come from 20 percent of your clients. And I do find that to be somewhat true. The trick is to have that 20 percent spread out as much as possible. In other words, I'm cautioning you against what I call the "one big client syndrome."

This is how many businesses get started. One big customer fills up six months of the calendar with work. Or one big project essentially provides a year's worth of business.

I once knew someone from one of my old jobs who quit his position with our mutual employer to "finally go out on his own" and start a home-based consulting business. Let's call him Joe. Joe basically got the guts to do this because he was assured of a plum contract from a big client in his industry right away.

Joe kicked butt for almost a year. The work from this one client was never-ending. It appeared that striking out on his own was a great thing — the money just rolled in. He was very happy at his success, and thought himself to be a good, solid businessman.

But was he? Or did he just get lucky, his success an illusion?

Had he learned anything at all about running a business? Did he have other clients? Did he network to find more clients, or market himself?

The truth is, he had no other clients, and knew next to nothing about running a business. In fact, Joe didn't even advertise or have any promotional materials — he said he didn't need them. He had one client. In other words, he essentially had a job.

Here on paper, you can see where this is going, can't you? But you know, this isn't so easy to see when you are Joe and someone is willing to pay you for your services (New Business Blinders again). Of course, the predictable thing happened — the project finally ended, Joe's client shook his hand for a job well done, and everyone was expected to move on. Except Joe really had nowhere to go. Here he was in business, and his meal ticket dried up. He had no idea what to do. It was almost like getting fired from a job. Except that business clients are harder to get than new jobs. Joe floundered for a bit, then bit the bullet and got himself another regular job, his brief fling with entrepreneurship over.

Sadly, this happens all the time. And it doesn't only happen to small companies, either — many larger companies would go under without their largest account. That's a bad way to conduct business.

Resistance Is Futile — or Is It?

I admit, it's very hard to resist giving all of your time to the big client if they want it. How can you logically turn down (or limit) a paying client? Especially if yes, you do have the time available.

My advice in this situation is to resist. Sure, take on the client, but only give them so many hours *even if your other hours are free.* If you truly want a *business*, you are going to have to spend time *on* your business, and you are going to have to build your client base. You can't do that if you have one big client that you give all your time to. *If you have one client, what you have is a job, not a business.* Which is okay if that's what you want, but don't ever fool yourself into thinking you're a successful businessperson — you aren't. You're working on contract for a company.

I practice what I preach. I have one large client now, and they could be larger if I wanted them to be. But in doing such, I'd have to shut everyone else out and just do work for this one client. Which might be great for a year. Or two. Or whatever length of time they keep supplying me with work.

But I've been around the block. I've seen businesses change direction, companies go out of business, and I've been asked to leave the premises several times. I know for a fact that almost all business relationships end. Be it the sale of a company, someone going out of business, new management, the boss's kid taking over, whatever … sooner or later, there's going to be that "Dan, we decided to go in another direction" phone call.

And yes, this can happen to anyone. Don't think, "Oh, XYZ corporation would never do that to me — they *love* me." They might love you (actually, I doubt the feeling is truly "love." It's probably more along the lines of "just friends"), but what if *they* lose their biggest customer? And cuts have to be made? Hard decisions like this are made every day, and the dollar always wins.

So I don't block out my calendar for *anyone.* Since I'm always ready for that phone call, I don't base my livelihood or my mortgage payment on any one client. Of course, it would hurt if my biggest client left me. I'd rather they didn't. But it would not hurt *nearly* to the extent it would if I filled up my calendar with just one client.

To be honest, I'd rather have unbilled hours, hours that I'll spend working *on* my business to try and get more clients, rather than filling up my entire calendar with one client. Naturally, I'm talking long term here. Almost any of my clients can get my full attention for a week or two, or for a short project. No problem at all.

Resist the siren song of the big client. While the short-term gain might be worth it, it will always sting in the long run. In the end, I'd rather have ten $500 clients than one $5,000 client.

Samples 6 and 7 are graphic representations of the possible revenue divisions among a business's clients.

SAMPLE 6
PERCENT OF BUSINESS — ONE DOMINANT CLIENT

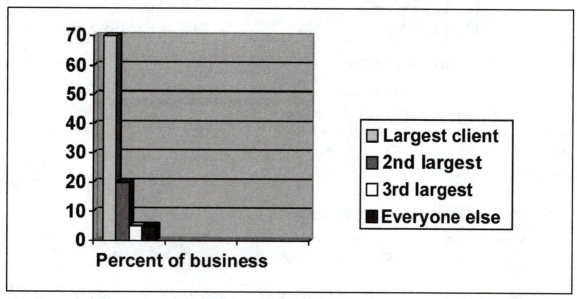

This chart shows a business where one client accounts for 70 percent of the revenue. This is never a good thing, because if this client drops you, you're in huge trouble.

SAMPLE 7
PERCENT OF BUSINESS — HEALTHY MIX

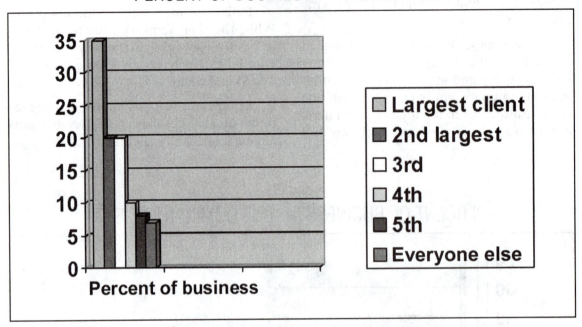

This chart shows a healthy mix of client ratios. The largest client accounts for 35 percent of revenue, which is not unusual for a home-based business. In addition, the top three clients account for just 75 percent of the revenue.

A LETHAL ASPECT OF THE 80/20 RULE

I have a friend who makes a decent living selling new products on a popular online auction site. He's a big-time seller, has a garage full of inventory, and ships out merchandise every day.

One day, he broke one of the auction site's rules, and they suspended him. Which completely shut him down. I mean *completely*. This is akin to having a store in a mall, and having the mall evict you. It's actually worse, because at least the store can open up across the street from the mall and still remain accessible to the local traffic. There is no "across the street" on the Internet.

My friend eventually got back on the auction site, but I hope that experience scared him enough to at least have a few other revenue streams. And I hope this little story got you thinking if you have a similar business model.

Chapter 38

MONEY TALKS (OR DOING BUSINESS ON A HANDSHAKE IS STUPID, AND OTHER INVOICING ISSUES)

Rick still owes me money.

Back in 1992, I sold Rick space in my direct-mail coupon pack. Rick owned a car wash and seemed to be eager to be included in my mailer. And since I was broke at the time, I was happy making the sale. Too happy, in fact. In order to spur business, I not only discounted my product, I took orders without a deposit. I just wanted to "make a sale."

Rick was an easy sale — and why wouldn't he be? Here I was, selling him space in my coupon pack, charging him nothing, telling him I'd bill him later. My coupon pack came out, Rick got lots of business from my coupon, and then promptly ignored my invoice. I can't get too mad about him ignoring my invoice because

Rick was pretty much broke too. Oh, the car wash looked busy, but he was going through a divorce, had tax troubles, etc.

Phone calls went unanswered, and when I went to see him, he told me he never got my invoice ... so I handed him one. The next time I went to see him, he wouldn't come out of his office. I was told to come back another time.

Eventually, I somewhat settled with Rick — I got free car washes. But you have to wash your car a lot of times before you reach several hundred dollars' worth. Add in the fact that my car was an old rust bucket, and something always fell off when I went through the car wash (not to mention the leaky windshield), and you can easily surmise that I didn't collect on the bill. I would have much preferred making a bartering arrangement with a defaulting beer store.

To be honest, I had a *lot* of nonpayment issues in my first business (which in turn led to my printer having the same problem with *me*), and I now realize that the fault was almost entirely mine. I've since gotten a lot smarter about how I invoice and do business, and I have cut my nonpayment issues to almost nil. In fact, while I've issued hundreds and hundreds of invoices over the last six years, I can count the number of nonpayers on one hand.

Invoicing Advice

The whole Rick situation (and others like it) really could have been prevented on my end. Let me outline some preventative measures.

If you are desperate for business, you are more apt to have invoicing issues

This is pretty simple, really — desperation for a buck leads one to do silly things, like doing business with questionable people just because you need work. Or doing business without a deposit or retainer. People are always more willing to say yes when no money is involved. This is a paradox, really, as the very type of client that will be swayed by "no deposit required" is *exactly* the type of client you want to stay away from.

If you do not have a strong relationship with a client, always get a deposit or prepayment

Anyone truly interested in your services will have no trouble paying a deposit. I get a 50 percent deposit before I do any work at all. And if the project will cost under $1,000, I take full prepayment (I don't want to be chasing anyone for $200).

I'm so strict about this that I don't even put people on my schedule until I get a deposit. Since I book my time out up to a month in advance, I *have* to do this. And I do not offer refunds if the project falls through or whatnot (although if someone runs into an issue and has to cancel, I'll credit all unused monies toward future work).

I learned something over the years: Many clients are great at saying, "Yes, I want you to do X." But if I don't take a deposit to cement the project, I find a great number of people who say yes end up not going through with the project for one reason or another. The deposit/prepayment is the binding ingredient. It separates true clients from pretenders.

And trust me when I tell you, good clients have no problem at all with this arrangement. They *expect* to pay a deposit. So get one.

Now, there are some exceptions to getting a deposit. If I develop a good relationship with a client, deposits eventually become unnecessary — I'll just invoice them monthly. And if a company like Microsoft calls me, I'll probably take my chances and forgo the deposit and just take their purchase order number.

A deposit ensures the client actually *wants* the work done

I recall one time when I did business with a manager who acted beyond his authority. He said yes to my coupon pack, but the company owner wasn't notified. Suffice it to say, the owner didn't want to be in my coupon pack. I got a big fat "We never authorized this ... oh, Dave authorized it? Dave doesn't have the power to do that. Sorry."

And, of course, to save his job, Dave told the owner he never authorized such a thing, and that I overstepped my bounds in assuming they wanted the coupon. I never got paid.

A deposit helps you avoid the string-along client

In addition to what I've already outlined, I cannot count the number of times a client has said, "Yes, I want you to do work — I'm just not ready yet. But hold space for me" — only to pull out when the time came. Or they keep saying "come back next week" or "after I get my car fixed, we'll do business," or something similar. Home-based businesses seem to run into this a lot. I have to tell you, that string-along client really doesn't want your service; he or she is just too timid to actually say no to you.

As I mentioned, I solve this problem by not putting anyone on my schedule without seeing money. Exceptions are made for long-term clients, but that's it. Money talks — everything else is fluff. And I don't chase. I may follow up once or twice, but after that, I consider whatever verbal agreements there were null and void.

If you follow these pointers, your life will be a lot easier in terms of collecting on invoices. Requiring a deposit also makes you more professional, and, believe it or not, commands a bit of respect. Clients know you are serious when you take a deposit.

Forget the handshake. Forget someone who says their word is good. Someone's word may be good, but a check is better.

Additional Invoicing Tips

If you can, invoice twice a month

I don't mean invoice clients twice a month, I mean choose two days a month (like the first and the 15th) when you will send out invoices. Keep some clients on a first of the month schedule, and others on the 15th. This helps with cash flow, and makes it seem like you are always getting checks.

Recognize that some clients take time to pay

The general rule of thumb is the bigger the client, the longer you will wait for your money. Most companies and people I do business with pay invoices in 30 or 60 days. Most corporations are like that. However, a little communication up front can make you aware of this. I have no problem waiting 60 days — as long as it's consistent, and I actually get paid in 60 days. You should establish payment terms up front.

Address Payment Issues Right Away

I always give a week's grace. If an invoice is marked 30 days, I give it another week. If there's still no check after the week's grace, I typically send a friendly email saying, "Could you check on invoice X and let me know its status." In almost every case, a check appears a few days later.

However, sometimes this doesn't work. This can be especially troublesome if I'm still doing work for the client (and thereby racking up more billable hours). I don't want to lose a client by stopping work because they are a few days late, but I don't want to rack up too many hours, either. So I have a limit — 30 days past due. In other words, I bill August 1st for work done in July. It's due August 31st. If October 1st rolls around and that August 1st invoice still isn't paid, I stop work for that client and (nicely but firmly) demand we get caught up. That's it — I can't let any more billable hours accumulate. If an invoice is a full month past due, obviously there's a problem, and it needs to be cleared up.

I've read in other books about businesses with invoices 120 days late; I don't know what kinds of businesses these people are running, but I need a better cash flow than that. I simply cannot afford to let hours accumulate while not getting paid. And I doubt you can either. Thirty days late is enough for me. I start the late notices then, and if I'm still doing work for the client, work stops until we're caught up.

And here's an ugly truth I have learned: If your invoicing problems are not solved quickly, it is almost always for one reason only — the client doesn't have the money.

Don't get emotionally involved with nonpayers

Since they have personal contact with clients, often owners of home-based businesses get a sob story when payment is late. Ninety-nine times out of 100, failure to pay is not a temporary thing, so be very wary in extending credit for someone going through a rough patch. Rough patches seldom get better right away (I've been through a few myself). The overwhelming likelihood is you will not get paid. Stick to my 30-day rule.

Tips to minimize nonpayment

I'd like to be able to give you a surefire way to collect on unpaid invoices, but unfortunately, none exists. Your chances of collecting on that long-past-due invoice are fairly remote. Even if you do get a court judgment, there is no enforcement of payment. Your likelihood of collecting goes down even further if the client is not local. (Let's face it: You aren't traveling six states to collect $1,100.)

This is why my 50 percent deposit (or full prepayment) and "30 days late" policies are all the more important. If I have half the bill paid up front, well, at least I don't lose too much. Yes, it's still a loss, but it's much easier to stomach than if I only took 20 percent down. And the 30-days policy ensures I won't rack up too many hours that will go unpaid.

COLLECTION TIP

If you are owed more than one invoice (such as two months' worth of invoices), insist on them being paid with separate checks. This way, if there's only some money in the account, one might clear and you'll at the least get something. I just had this happen to me. A client owed me two months' worth of invoices, and I asked for a check for each. One cleared, the other bounced. If both amounts were on one check, the whole thing would have bounced.

It's still up in the air what's going to happen with this client, but no matter what happens, I'm very happy I at least got one payment out of the two.

Never get angry or make threats

When someone owes me money and won't pay, my first instinct is to show up at their doorstep and say, "Pay, or else ..." Then I calm down and realize that, despite the incredible creature comforts offered, I do not want to be charged with assault and sent to jail. But I admit, not getting angry is hard to do.

When owed money, the best way to handle it is with professional communication — be it a letter or a phone call. The biggest threat you should make is, "I'm sorry, but I'm going to have to turn this over to my attorney." Screaming, yelling, threatening, or anything else like that is completely out of the question. It's unprofessional. Hard-headed bullies yell. Professional business-people do not.

Again, clients who don't pay are in the scant minority. And I *do* mean scant. But the way I do business (requiring a deposit, prepayment, not acting desperate, using a calm collection technique) ensures I have mostly good clients.

Chapter 39

BARTERING

There are two things I'd like to mention about bartering. The first thing is it's a very viable way of doing business at times. I have always liked bartering. In fact, most people do.

The second thing I'd like to say about it is to be careful. Because it is so universally liked, it's easy to barter more than you need to, and end up with nothing to pay bills with. I found this out the hard way. Trust me, credit card companies aren't as enthusiastic about bartering as the rest of us are. They'd much rather have the money.

What Is Bartering?

Bartering is simply a trading of goods and/or services. I perform my service for you or give you goods, and you perform your service for me or give me goods. It works very well in many situations.

Say you have a daycare, and are looking to have a new front porch built. One of your clients is a carpenter. You agree to trade X number of weeks of daycare services for the carpenter to build you a new porch. This way, you both get services without laying out money. You don't lay out any money for a new porch, and the carpenter gets a few weeks/months without paying for daycare. But be sure to ask your accountant how to handle bartering for tax purposes.

I recently did a barter deal where I traded my writing services with a web designer I am friends with. I wrote a few pages of copy for her new website, and she created a working template for a new website for me to use. It was great for both of us — I got a needed service, so did she, and money did not have to change hands.

The key word I just wrote is *needed*. Bartering is a great way to do business from time to time, but it only really works well if the services are truly needed. It's very easy to barter way more than is financially feasible. Bartering is sometimes an illusion — yes, you are doing business, but are you generating income?

In my first business, I bartered a *lot*. I did it because, well, I was broke. So one of the first things I did was barter one of my direct-mail coupons with a deli. I got a $300 credit at the deli, and the deli got a coupon in my direct-mail pack. Okay, so now my lunch was taken care of — you could say this was a needed service.

However, my next barter deal wasn't so needed. I bartered new tires for my car. Well, my car didn't really need tires yet (the tires were about the only decent part of the car), but I, under the illusion of "Hey, business is business," decided to go ahead with it (it was the only way this merchant would participate in my coupon pack). I then ran into another merchant — a butcher — who wanted to barter instead of paying me.

"Well, what enterprising young man doesn't need some fine steaks?" I thought to myself (myself who already has $300 worth of credit at the deli). I went through with that deal as well.

All told, out of 30 coupons sold, about ten were sold by bartering. A full third of my revenue wasn't really money. But I had tires. And steaks. And I got my laundry done for free. And you already know about the car wash that I was afraid to take my car through. In addition, I had $300 worth of pet food, which would probably last me years, since I only had one skinny cat. I also had credit for $300 worth of lighting fixtures … why I thought I would need $300 worth of lighting in my apartment, I'll never know. But again, the merchant asked about bartering, so under the ruse of "business is business," I did it.

On top of all the other mistakes I made, you could say I bartered my way out of business. Because when it came time to pay the bills, my landlord was not interested in cat food.

So be careful with bartering. It's great if you truly need the product or service, but don't get carried away and use bartering as a means to do business.

Chapter 40

SMOKING

I'm sure you find it a bit odd that I have a chapter on smoking in a business book. But, as a former (heavy) smoker, I now see smoking in a very different light. Essentially, since I joined the other side, I have adopted their highbrow, carefully crafted, and gracefully worded mantra: Smoking sucks. I have also perfected the highly exaggerated "fake cough" whilst waving my hand to clear away the smoke. Yes, I have become an annoying nonsmoker.

So I will say this as tactfully as I can: In very simple terms, smoking will almost certainly cost you business.

I know, I know … it's not fair. And it's nobody's business whether you smoke or not. I get it.

But get this: Roughly 75 percent of the US population do not smoke. Studies also seem to indicate that the more educated you are, and the more money you make, the less likely you are to smoke. So the people with money — those customers that you *really* want — overwhelmingly don't smoke. Okay, so I brought up statistics and vague studies to make a point. You should be aware, though, that most people simply don't smoke; smoking is a turnoff to a majority of the population. By and large, non-smokers *do not like smoking.* And they do not like smokers. Period.

I guarantee you, if you smoke, your smoking habit will interfere with your interactions with clients.

For example, I had a building company look at a job at my house. I was outside breathing the decidedly fresh air when I saw the truck pull up, so I walked over to greet the workers and show them the work I needed done. I guess the company rule was "no smoking in the truck," because as soon as the guys arrived, they exited the truck and *immediately* lit up. I mean, before even returning my greeting, both guys had to get that cigarette lit and take a puff. The way I saw it, instead of two competent, friendly guys greeting me, two demons emerged from a plume of smoke.

Yeah, we nonsmokers tend to exaggerate a bit, but then again, I was the customer, and we're always right. If I saw demons, they were demons.

It really put me off and got us started on the wrong foot. In fact, the conversation never really recovered, and they did not get the job. Yes, they lost it partly because they smoked as soon as they got out of the truck. I know it's unfair. Tough.

Now, smokers (again, of which I was one) will call me shallow and say that smoking is no indication of a person's ability to do a job, and on the surface, I will agree with that. But the fact remains that your specialized skill is but a small part of the business process — other skills like people skills, sales skills, etc., all come into play. And having that cigarette dangling from your lips gives you a solid F in the people skills department. It also gives you an F in the "not arriving smelling foul" department (which is one of the more important departments in business).

And yes, when you smoke, you do stink.

Tell me, why do you shower? Really — answer the question. Why is it important to be clean? Would you go in front of your customers smelling of yesterday's day at the pig fair (assuming you attended)? Of course you wouldn't. So why would you go smelling of smoke? And you *do* smell of smoke. You don't think you do because you are immune to it, but to nonsmokers, you reek *long* after you finish your cigarette. And no, putting down the car window doesn't help.

Plus, there's the time factor.

When I hire someone, I do not want to see them take an hourly cigarette break. I'm paying you to do a job, not smoke. I know it's only a few minutes, but let's do a little math: It takes about seven minutes to smoke a cigarette. Fair enough? Multiply that by a pack (20 cigarettes), and you have 140 minutes. That's two hours and 20 minutes spent smoking if you smoke a pack a day. I have to tell you, I don't know of many successful businesspeople who have two-plus hours a day to waste. Even if you work alone at home, taking time to smoke will hurt you.

And if you smoke while you work, it also makes me think you don't really have your mind on your job, and it also runs other risks, as I'll point out in this quick anecdote: Once, I hired a tree-pruning company to trim a massive oak in my yard. I was watching them work, and the guy in the cherry-picker bucket was smoking as he worked the chainsaw 50 feet off the ground.

This reminded me of something. When I hung out at the bar years ago, I liked to shoot pool. And it was always deemed "cooler" to shoot with a cigarette hanging out of your mouth. However, there was one huge drawback — every so often, this "cool" habit made smoke go in your eyes as you shot, ruining whatever shot you had planned. So I stopped doing it. That's also about the time in my life when I learned that looking cool is pretty dumb in the adult world.

I tell this story because when I had a pool cue in my hand, I risked missing the eight ball. This schmuck trimming my tree had a *chainsaw* in his hands, and he was throwing down heavy pieces of tree limbs onto my property. And sure enough, when the trimming was done, there was damage: an expensive little Japanese maple I had planted a year earlier (which I had clearly pointed out for them to avoid) was ruined, and a garden light was also broken. I called the company owner and told him I was deducting $200 from the bill. I also told him about the smoking, and mentioned that perhaps that was why the damage occurred. He reluctantly agreed.

I think I know why not smoking on the job is an issue for some people. Not too long ago, smoking was widely accepted. When I was a kid in the '70s, it seemed like *everyone* smoked *everywhere*, and they smoked *all the time*. At the mall, at the supermarket, at offices, even the teachers at school … everywhere you looked, people were smoking. I'll bet the doctor who delivered me in 1966 bummed a cigarette from my mother.

But in the last ten years, this has really changed. And you need to change too. I'm not telling you to quit, but during the business day, even if you work alone at home, don't smoke. Unless you want to lose business.

Part 3
SOUL

Chapter 41

A SUREFIRE WAY TO GET YOUR SPOUSE OR PARTNER ON BOARD

One of the toughest parts of any business venture is getting the approval and support of your spouse or partner (I mean partner as in unmarried or live-in partner, not business partner). This is especially true for entrepreneurs starting out, as you are usually starting from scratch and are taking on at least a small amount of financial risk. Also, many businesses simply cannot be run part time, so you might have to quit a job to make a go of it.

And, truth be told, financial risks (even small ones) and quitting jobs are not things most spouses or partners smile upon. Nobody ever says, "You're going to quit your job and deprive us of your income? So you can start your own business? Oh my goodness, this is a dream come true! I *knew* that somehow, someway, the financially irresponsible side of your personality would emerge! I'm *so happy*! Let's go out to eat and celebrate!"

No, that never happens. In fact, those words have never been uttered. Ever.

Instead, here are some of the typical phrases uttered in a "I want to start a business" argument:

- "You don't believe in me."
- "You have no foresight."
- "You're always against my dreams."
- "I *do too* know what I'm doing."
- "Just for one minute look at the big picture."

And so on. If you've ever discussed your business plans with your spouse or partner, you have probably articulated at least one of the above.

Now, before I tell you how to get your spouse's support, I'm going to tell you that without it, you are likely sunk. You will not succeed in business if your spouse/partner is standing there cross-armed after the first week saying "Okay, Mr./Mrs. Trump … where's the big bucks?" Almost all businesses start slowly, and you will never survive the start-up period if the closest person to you is against your efforts.

So, in essence, you *must* get your spouse or partner on board. Here's how you do it: You make some money first.

It's true — that's all you have to do. Somehow, someway, you need to *prove* that you can make money. I don't care how, but you need to demonstrate that you are capable of bringing in an income on your own. It goes a *long* way in alleviating your spouse's fears and concerns. Money simply has that power.

Let me give you an example, because I have a lot of experience here.

In my past relationships, most of my exes would roll their eyes every time I had a new business idea. My business ventures were usually met with scorn, even though I told them of the money I'd eventually make. In many discussions, I uttered many of the phrases you just read. I could not understand it. Didn't they *want* to break out of the day-to-day routine and actually run a business? I sure did, and I had a burning desire to do *something*. Why couldn't anyone just share my vision?

I now realize why. I never gave anyone a reason to. It's as simple as that.

Not one of my exes had any reason to believe *anything* I said about making money and running a business because I hadn't proven that I could make a dime. Heck, I couldn't even hold a steady job for most of my life, yet there I was, claiming I could somehow make big bucks in business.

See, the truth is, *I knew* I could/would make it in business. I always knew I'd be successful, just like I always knew I'd write a book. I believed in myself wholeheartedly. But my flaw was I didn't give *them* any reason to believe in me.

Now, had I came home one day and said, "Here sweetie, here's $500 I made fixing computers last Saturday," do you think I would have been viewed differently (especially since I used the word *sweetie*)? We'll never know, because I didn't try to make any money at all. I just wanted them to believe on pure faith, which is really asking a lot when the rent is involved. It's asking too much, now that I think about it.

Because the simple truth was, I could have tried to make some money before approaching any of my exes with my ideas. Heck, if I wanted to start a computer repair business, what was stopping me from beating the street on a Saturday and trying to get a little work? But, I didn't do it, so I never really had their support.

But things changed for me.

Fast forward a few years — I'm now married to my wife, Maryellen. I was working at a nice company doing e-commerce programming (Maryellen, upon meeting me, commented on how it was so nice to actually date a guy with a good job ... of course, lucky for me she didn't know my work history).

So here I am at this good job, and I'm starting to have entrepreneurial thoughts. This time, I keep them to myself, because they always got me yelled at in the past. However, one day, I get a call from a company in Florida. They saw my postings in an online forum dedicated to the specific piece of e-commerce programming software I used for my job (I used to answer people's questions on how to use it). The Florida company figured I could help them with their e-commerce programming, since they used the same software. I agreed to help them via email in my spare time (for a fee, of course).

The very next day, I got into an argument with my boss and was fired from my job (again). Maryellen was a little nervous, because hey, we needed my salary, so this was a big deal. I toyed with the idea of approaching her about my not looking for a job and instead doing something on my own, but first I had the Florida company that I had to do this job for. I did the job, sent them the work via email, emailed them an invoice, and two weeks later, as if by magic, a check for $1,500 was in the mailbox.

And it *really was* like magic. Instead of me asking Maryellen about going into business for myself, she flat-out *told* me to do it. She liked $1,500 checks arriving in the mail, and wanted more of them. I must confess, I did too.

So I set up shop doing freelance programming for the software I was proficient in, and I haven't looked back. Throughout it all, with freelance programming eventually turning into writing, she's been solidly behind me every step of the way, and has backed every business move I have made. She has 100 percent faith in me (thanks, sweetie!).

You see, my wife sees me not as a dreamer and schemer (which I kind of was during the time of my past relationships), but as someone who can really produce income. Why? *Because I actually did it.*

And that's the difference. If you want to succeed, you have to get your spouse on board. I know this firsthand. There are other reasons I've succeeded in my business (they're recounted throughout this book), but one of the most important is having your spouse or partner in your corner. I've done it both ways — believe me, having them behind you is *much* better. And the way to get them behind you is to *prove* to them that you are capable of making money.

So here's my advice: Make some money in whatever line of work you want to start a business in. If you want to have a web design business, make a few websites for local businesses. If you want to be a carpenter, go build a few decks on the weekend. Give the money to your spouse as a surprise. If your business is one you can't go make money at right away, instead open an eBay account and sell something.

Don't say anything, don't talk about it, and don't tell them of riches. And don't mention things like "dreams" and "someday" and ask them to see the big picture. *Go out and make some money* — be someone who produces income — and your spouse will be in your corner in a heartbeat.

Chapter 42

CHARGE A FAIR PRICE — FOR BOTH YOUR CUSTOMER AND YOU

One sure way to sabotage your business is to not charge enough for your product or service. This mistake happens all the time.

"Charge a fair price" … it really sounds simple, doesn't it? But it's not.

I think this is because deep down, most people are somewhat afraid to do this. I know I felt pangs of guilt when I charged a client over $1,000 for what amounted to a few hours of work. See, I was still conditioned to the job mentality that said "X dollars per hour." But the $1,000 I was charging was the going rate for the *result* I produced. It truly took me a little while to actually *believe* that what I did was worth that kind of money. Breaking out of this "hours mentality" is essential to your success.

Part of what helped me get over this was that my client happily paid and then immediately secured my services for another project. Apparently, I *was* worth the money.

Not believing that what you are doing is worth the money is a huge mistake, and can bury your business very quickly. It's a big reason so many entrepreneurs go out of business — they charge too little for their services and price themselves into oblivion. They do it under the guise of "fairness" and/or "not being greedy."

I know a (former) computer consultant who did exactly this. He started a business doing computer repairs and networking for local businesses. He charged $30 per hour. Now, I know that may sound like a lot to some people, but it is far too little to be charging when you own the business and are visiting people on-site. $75 to $100 per hour is more like the going rate today, and I don't know many businesses that would have a problem paying that fee. I told him he was making a big mistake, but my friend insisted he "wouldn't be greedy" and "I have to start small to build the business." So he charged $30 per hour.

My friend also seemed to do everything he could to *reduce* his bill — he'd constantly do small jobs and tell the client, "Oh, I won't charge for that"; or he'd have to go to the store to buy a new cable because the client's old one was worn, and wouldn't charge the client for his driving time; or he'd spend an hour with Sally, the slow-witted (but always pleasant) receptionist, painstakingly showing her the subtleties of the "double click," and not charge for it.

All seemingly nice stuff, but he barely paid the bills. He was terribly busy, too. People jumped on that cheap price, but he ran himself ragged, working his tail off for next to nothing. My friend would have been better off working a regular job.

In fact, that's exactly what happened. He's now out of business and back in a corporate cubical. He couldn't make a dime of profit, despite being pretty busy. Gee, I wonder why?

It is essential — ESSENTIAL — that you get paid a fair amount for what you do. That means pretty close to the going rate. If the computer consultants in your area charge $75 per hour, you need to charge right around that. If you make a product and it normally sells for about $20, you won't do yourself any favors by selling it for $12.99.

Giving away the store is fine if you can afford it. But don't start out that way.

But What If I'm Charging a Low Rate to Build the Business? Is That Okay?

No, it isn't. Charging a cheap price to "build the business" never works. Here's why.

When you charge a cheap rate, you can almost never raise it substantially for existing customers ever again. You cannot charge $30 per hour and then all of a sudden charge $75 per hour. So even if you *do* raise your rates for new customers, the old customers still pay the cheap rate. Let me tell you, you will *hate* doing work for them after a while.

I used to think I was underpaid at my "real" jobs. You probably do too. So why on earth would you undercut yourself when *you* are setting the price? It's bizarre that this happens. But it does. It happened to me, too.

When I first started my writing business, I charged a ridiculously low rate for every job — like $50 per page. It seemed like a lot of money at the time. I mean, seriously — *50 bucks* to write one stupid page? Where do I sign up?

Then I got a complicated 20-page job, and it was *really* a lot of work (lots of research, a tough topic, a demanding client, etc.). Took me almost two weeks. That's $1,000 for two weeks' work. That's $26k a year. I made that 15 years ago.

Hmmm … suddenly $50 a page isn't all that much money.

The trick is to not compare what you are charging with the salaries you made at your old jobs. $30 per hour is a decent salary at a "job." But it's *extremely* low when you own a business. Remember, a job paying you $30 an hour has to cover your rent, utilities, taxes, health care, maintenance, advertising, office equipment, etc. *Your* business will have to pay for those things too — on a smaller scale, likely, but it will still have to pay them.

So the rates you are charging are not all "salary." Never, ever forget this.

Don't Work for Free

There's another reason why "pricing yourself out of business" happens: Many starting entrepreneurs put almost no value on their own time.

Let me give you an example. Let's pretend you want to make custom birdhouses in the shape of a castle, and you sell them at a craft show on Saturdays. You figure out that wood, nails, and stain will cost you about $4 per birdhouse. You then get clever and factor in things like heat and electricity for the garage workshop, gas for trips to the store to buy materials, and other miscellaneous stuff. This adds another dollar to each birdhouse. Now we're up to five bucks to produce a birdhouse. Not too bad yet, right?

Then you factor in the rent on a craft fair booth ($75) and the trip there ($5 in gas), and make the assumption that if you sell your birdhouses for $20 each, you'll make a $15 profit. All you have to do is sell six birdhouses, and your profit clears the booth fee and gas. Pure profit after that! Selling six should be easy. Heck, you figure

you'll sell twice that. Maybe even three times.

And you do — in fact, you sell 21 birdhouses, for a gross of $420. Minus materials and garage expenses, you made $315. Minus the booth ($75) and gas there ($5), and you made $235. Not too shabby for one Saturday, right?

But wait — it took you 45 minutes to make each birdhouse (including staining them and cleanup). That's 15.75 hours of work for the 21 birdhouses you sold. Plus the eight hours at the craft fair. That's 23.75 hours so far. Two trips to the hardware store for materials is another two hours — now 25.75 hours now. Add one hour to set up and take down the craft fair booth, and add a half hour each way to and from the craft fair. Fair enough? We're up to 27.75 hours. For $235.

My friend, that's $8.47 an hour.

Now, let's add in the fact that you made these birdhouses in your garage after work — spending more than three hours a night, plus all day Saturday. Is this time *really* only worth $8.47 per hour to you?

Probably not.

I'm not saying that making birdhouses is a bad thing, but you are certainly not making "almost $300 on one Saturday," as many people would probably tell their friends. In fact, unless you *love* making birdhouses every night and spending all day Saturday at the craft fair, it's likely that you will quickly lose interest in selling birdhouses.

Sadly, people miscalculate their business costs *all* the time. They factor in costs, but *never* factor in their labor. I even had one friend tell me, "Why should I? My labor is free."

No, it isn't free.

You wouldn't work for someone else for free — why would you work for yourself for free? You must be fairly compensated, or you will struggle mightily in your business. In fact, you will soon *hate* your business if you are working for free.

So just charge a fair, competitive, and consistent rate.

How to Bill — Hourly versus Other Methods

Since this book addresses many types of home-based businesses, it's difficult for me to tell you how you should charge. Some businesses lend themselves better to charging by the hour (and your clients may expect it). For example, a lawyer usually bills by the hour. So might a computer technician. Or a plumber.

Others want to bill by the project. A contractor might quote a fixed price for an addition. Or a computer technician might quote a fixed price for networking an office. But there's nothing set in stone: a hair stylist usually charges by the haircut, but a specialized pro might charge by the hour. A daycare might charge by the child or by the week or by the hour.

So I can only offer you general advice on this. That being said, I personally find it preferable to charge by the project/service if at all possible. People seem to like this better (as they know exactly what they are paying up front), and it is usually more profitable for you. It might be okay to

charge by the hour if your hourly fees are more than $100 per hour, but anything under than that and you're getting into the job mentality. There's a general consensus among many successful entrepreneurs that charging by the hour means you just created yourself a "job," which is the very thing most successful entrepreneurs try to stay away from.

In addition, charging by the hour makes the client scrutinize your bill more closely. "Did you really work that many hours?" they'll ask. Also, they might start comparing *your* hourly rate to the rate they get at their own job (which isn't a fair comparison — they aren't paying the overhead you are). It's just messy in most cases. Charging by the project/job is much better.

Now, there are exceptions. For example, I charge one large client by the hour now, as I do work for them almost daily, and the projects are always different. Hourly is best for this particular client. But for everyone else, I charge by the project. This works best for me, and it seems to work best for most entrepreneurs that I talk to.

One Last Thing on Pricing

Many times a client will say something like, "Well, there will be a *lot* more work in the future. So can I get a better price?"

I always reply, "Sure, if the future work is indeed significant and warrants a quantity discount, I'll be happy to give you a better price on it. But this current job will have to be priced as is."

Listen: *Everybody* promises future work. Know how often that future work actually materializes? I'd say less than 5 percent of the time. Just food for thought.

Chapter 43

A HUGE MISTAKE PEOPLE MAKE IN MARKETING AND ADVERTISING

I'm going to discuss a particular advertising and marketing mistake in this section because it encompasses more than just a nuts and bolts "advertising mistake." It has more to do with perception and expectations than with a particular advertising or marketing strategy.

The easiest way to discuss this is to first ask you to think of a résumé.

What is the purpose of a résumé?

If you answered "to get a job" (or something similar), you're wrong. *Very* wrong, in fact. The résumé, by itself, has nothing to do with actually getting you a job.

Instead, the résumé gets you an *interview* from the employer you sent it to (or to be even more specific, it gets you the phone call that leads to an interview). The résumé, in and of itself, is completely useless in actually getting you the *job*. Yet, many people see it as a tool to help them secure a job, and write it that way. They have this big, encompassing résumé that goes over every possible aspect of their background, and they use the same one for all situations. Then they wonder why the phone doesn't ring.

The phone doesn't ring because a jerk like me came along and laser-focused his résumé to do nothing more than get a phone call from *that* company, for *that* job. I do that by making sure my résumé piques the particular reader's interest. Trust me, I know what I'm talking about — remember, I've been fired a dozen times, so if I know one thing, it's how to get a *new* job (if I only knew how to keep one …).

Too many people take this same "overall" approach with their advertising and marketing. They want every piece of advertising they do to go over every single reason someone should use them, and they almost expect the ad itself to do the selling. That almost never works (except for the sales/marketing proposal I talked about in Chapter 32).

Let's consider a Yellow Pages ad. What's the purpose of a Yellow Pages ad? Now, if you're paying attention and realize where I'm going with this, your answer will not be "to get business." Instead, the answer should be "to get a phone call or prospect."

And the ad should be written with that in mind. Forget filling your ad with silly one-liners that these ads are bursting with: "one call, that's all"; "at Putrid Plumbing, we treat you right"; "friendly service with a smile" (as opposed to what — a scowl? I don't understand why anyone would need to point out that they smile).

Instead, think of the audience who sees your ad, and *why* they are looking. Let me give you an example: Say you are a plumber. Now, there are two main reasons people will look for a plumber's ad — they have a remodeling/installation job they need done, or they have an emergency. So this probably is not the place to try and go after large, long-term contract work. By and large, nobody with a 24-month, $600,000 plumbing job will start with the Yellow Pages when looking for a plumber to fill that contract.

Instead, sweet Mrs. Turnberry will be looking. Ten to one, Mrs. Turnberry either wants a leaky pipe fixed (right now, as the floodwaters are rising), or she wants a new sink/toilet/tub installed. You know what Mrs. Turnberry wants from your ad? She wants to know you will come quickly, that you will do a good job, and that you are a professional. "Call us in an emergency," "in business since 1984," "fully insured," and "no job too small or too large" are good things to say in your ad. If you are licensed, say that, too.

Forget wasting space on "knowledgeable and reliable" or "service with a smile" — she really isn't going to read that and say "Hmm, I like a smiling plumber." Again, smiling (and saying so in print) is probably not going to tip the scales in your favor. Personally, I'd much prefer a scowling plumber who came right now.

The lesson from this example can be applied to almost any business. Above all else, make sure you address the clientele reading your ad and the most likely reason they are reading.

In addition, keep your ad neat: a few bullet points, maybe one phrase or so, but keep it neat and "open." But always remember *why* you are advertising, *who* is reading, and *why* they are reading.

It's really as simple as "address your reader's needs." Put yourself in your client's shoes and ask, "What do they want in a [*insert your business here*]?" Then offer what they want.

Chapter 44

ONCE OPENED, DOORS TEND TO STAY OPEN

This is a quick word of warning about how you do business with people. I allude to this in other chapters of the book, but I'll be crystal clear here: In a home-based business, once you open a door for someone, in most cases, you can never close it.

This means once you give a discount, you're expected to always give a discount. Once you give someone special treatment or go out of your way for someone, it's almost expected. It's like a lawyer looking for a precedent — once you establish a precedent, there's no going back. Let's look at a few examples of what I mean.

Rush Jobs

This is a sticky spot for many home-based business owners because we want to please people — we want to be someone clients can count on in an emergency. When a client calls with a rush job, however, it almost always puts a strain on you. And I'm here to tell you that once you do a rush job for someone, and don't charge a premium fee for doing so, watch out. I'm not saying you can't, or even shouldn't. But watch out.

I have had a few clients that call and ask for something *right now*. I remember one in particular that had a big meeting "tonight" and needed a thank-you letter. And although my normal lead time for new work is almost always two to three weeks, I did the rush job at no extra charge.

But I noticed something. The next job this client had for me was needed in a hurry too. And the next. All of a sudden, my usual two-to-three-week lead time was nonexistent with this client. He expected every job fairly quickly. Now it's not that this client had all kinds of big meetings that cropped up out of nowhere — he just followed basic human nature and wanted his projects done as soon as possible, and since I had set a precedent without any issue ...

Similar things would happen almost every time I took on a rush job. All of a sudden, because I could do it once, they thought I could always do it. It's *very* hard to say no once you've established that yes, you *will* drop everything for them.

I've learned how to handle this, however.

I now charge an extra fee for rush work, depending on how big the job is, and how busy I am. And I use it in all but the most extreme cases. This is not about the money, but about respect for my time. If I charge a client 25 to 50 percent extra for a rush job, it lets them know I am busy, and my time is valuable. It's a reminder that no, this is *not* the norm.

Of course, exceptions can always be made. I don't recommend getting your one special client angry for no good reason. I also make exceptions for *true* emergencies. However, I have found that true emergencies are few and far between. You'd be surprised at how many "I need this ASAP" people really *don't* need it ASAP. I recall one guy who needed a letter "right away." I dropped everything and did it, and then asked a week later how it was received by the person he sent it to. He replied, "Oh, I haven't sent it out yet." Lucky for him I don't have Jedi mind powers, because my thoughts were not pleasant.

Discounts

I'm not a big fan of offering discounts for no good reason. The personal nature of a home-based business makes offering one-time discounts difficult. Big impersonal businesses and retail stores can get away with seasonal specials, promotions, etc. But the minute you give someone a discount in a home-based business, you've just established a new price point with this customer.

And people will ask for discounts. People (especially new clients) think it's just fine to negotiate with a home-based business-person. "Can you do a little better?" I'm sometimes asked. "I'm sorry, but those are my fees. I feel my rates are fair for the quality of work I do," is my usual answer. Most of the time, I get the job anyway.

Introductory Rates

I mentioned in the chapter on advertising (Chapter 33) that I used to sell Yellow Pages ads, and that these companies are notorious for offering new advertisers great rates. One of the things we salespeople *hated* was calling on these advertisers for the *second* year. That's because their rate went *way* up — sometimes quadrupling. More often than not, the customer either canceled the ad, or cut *way* down on the size. Since it was a sales-based business, anything other than our customer renewing at the new rate meant a stern lecture from our sales manager, who was one of those type-A idiots who said things like, "NO doesn't really mean NO. It means, 'Give me more information.'"

Incidentally, this always confused me. To me, used in the context I'm describing, no means something akin to "No, I don't want it. Now go away." In fact, I once made the mistake of breaking out Webster's Dictionary and reading the meaning of the word *no* aloud at one of our countless (and utterly pointless) sales meetings. It livened the mood, but to say the sales manager was not amused is a huge understatement (are you beginning to see why I've been fired so many times?).

Anyway, my point is, a low introductory rate is *the* rate in most clients' eyes. Raising it and keeping the client happy is very, very hard. This doesn't mean you can't raise your rates — most businesses do every few years. But these are small, expected increases, not a low introductory rate and then a big jump in rates.

As I mentioned earlier, if you have some clients locked into a low rate, you will eventually *hate* doing work for them — no matter how loyal they are or how long you've worked for them. When you can make a lot more money doing work for other clients, you will begin to resent it when your discounted client calls.

Chapter 45

AN ASPECT OF WORKING AT HOME THAT YOU MAY FIND ANNOYING

This is for those of you who will be spending a lot of time actually *at* home in your home-based business. There's one super-annoying aspect of it that isn't very obvious to the outside world, but is something you are going to have to deal with. It's not the isolation, or no coworkers, or requirement of self-motivation. It has nothing to do with kids, dogs, or getting distracted by the TV.

It's about respect. Plain and simple respect.

See, when you work at home, most people don't think you really work. Not like they think you would if you went to a job every day. This goes for spouses, extended family, neighbors … everyone, really.

Understanding and supportive as she is, it took my wife a little while before she understood that I actually work *harder* than if I had a job. Oh, on the surface she knew. But there were times in the beginning when she'd ask me to run an errand during the day, and if I said I couldn't, she might say something like, "But you're home all day — can't you pick something up from the store for me?"

Now, I understand she mostly meant, "Since you don't have to ask the boss to leave, could you pick it up?" But the way it comes out, the "you're home all day" is somewhat condescending, and it kind of invites conflict. Let's just say I know how a lot of stay-at-home mothers feel in this regard.

Yes, I'm home all day, and I'm working most of it.

Friends and neighbors too think, "Gee, it must be nice to be home all day." Yes, it is nice, but that's because I have the self-discipline to make it work. However, I do agree that viewed from the outside, it must seem idyllic. But step inside my office and sit with me for a few days, and you'll see something different.

Even some other home-based business owners think if you work *in* the home that it's more of a hobby or a "side business" than a real business. A roofer working in the November cold will not see you as an equal in terms of owning and running a business. And it took my family a few years before "how's your side business?" became "how's business?"

Yes, I can get up and leave when I want, and I can go to the store if I want as well (this is one of the advantages I listed way back in Chapter 8). But that doesn't mean I can leave *on demand*. I remember one day when our dog had to go to the vet in the morning due to a slight emergency. I told my wife I couldn't bring the dog because I had a lot of work to do. So she brought the dog herself (she was off that day). Later in the day, when I finished what I was working on, I announced I had to go to the store. She said, "Wait, I thought you had a lot of work?"

She was a bit put off. All she could see was that I was too busy to help in the morning, but now I had time to go to the store in the afternoon. How could I go to the store? Didn't I have a lot of work?

I had to explain that yes, at the time that the dog needed to go to the vet, I could not break away. It's like telling your coworker you can't help with something because you're busy. Does that mean you can't help them in the afternoon? Of course not.

After explaining it like that, she understood. And believe me, she already was very understanding. But during the first few years, she still sometimes fell into the trap of, "well, you're home — you can do your work anytime."

Trust me, this is no longer an issue for me. I really don't care if anyone apart from my wife thinks I do nothing. But it definitely *used* to bother me, and it will probably bother you in the beginning as well. I used to get annoyed when someone would say, "You work at home? Boy, you're lucky. That must be so easy." I wanted so badly to tell them luck had little to do with it — and it was hard work, etc. Their comments irritated me.

I've since learned to be more confident in my business ability and to be proud of my work (which of course people are going to think is easy), so I don't get annoyed anymore. When people say, "Boy, you're lucky," I just smile and say, "Yes, I enjoy it a lot."

Just be aware that people will perceive you differently, and roll with it.

Chapter 46

DAYS OFF AND VACATIONS

The classic example of the entrepreneur is the person who works 12 hours a day, seven days a week to get the business going. And it's true that most businesses require a *lot* of effort to get off the ground.

Even my business, where I sit at a desk in my basement, took a Herculean effort to get going. It took me a month just to build my first website, never mind setting up the credit card processing, making sure the advertising was in place, writing and releasing a few press releases, etc. This is without doing any client work. Then, as the work started to come in, I still had plenty to do. I set up a second credit card processor, I developed new services and increased the website, I got my business listed with the BBB and put their seal on my website —

lots of stuff. I pretty much worked every single day.

And after a while, I was tired. I mean, I was really burned out. Maryellen had to step in and literally *demand* that I slow down and not only take some time off, but achieve a better work/life balance.

Know what I found out? I work better, and actually get more done, when I take some time off. In talking with many fellow entrepreneurs, a nice balance between work and time off serves them well also. You too would be well served by making sure you do the same. Now, I'm not talking about hours in a day — I still often work 10 to 12 hours a day (and some days I work 6 hours). I'm talking about days off and vacations.

I own a business for several reasons: I like to do things my way; I like being free; and I want a better quality of life than nine-to-five in an office affords me. Well, you know what a better quality of life *isn't*? It's working your fingers to the bone. I know this flies in the face of what many entrepreneurs will tell you, but at some point, you have to step back and start treating yourself *better* than if you had a top-flight job.

Because, in the end, isn't that why you wanted to do things your way in the first place?

At this point, for me, this means taking every weekend and most holidays off (I use the bank as my guide — if the bank is closed, I'm closed). I also grab an occasional "mental health day" when I can squeeze it in (usually on a Friday). And since last year, I bumped my vacation to four weeks a year (taken in four time periods — I usually take one week off each season).

And while to some people this may seem a little extravagant, it's not much different than what many working people get, especially at the executive level. Well, in your own company, *you're* the chief executive.

Now, I do not suggest you adopt a schedule like mine in the beginning — I certainly didn't. But I do suggest you start out with one nonnegotiable day off a week (two if you can swing it). Make it any day you want (Sunday works nicely), but make sure you take it off every week. Also, take the major holidays off — most clients do not expect you to work Christmas or New Year's Day anyway.

And while I don't suggest four weeks vacation in the beginning, I do recommend a few Friday-to-Monday long weekends the first year. Even if all you do is sit around the house.

> **As soon as you are able, grab more time off. Yes, entrepreneurs often have to be told to do this.**

I've learned something: Time off is precious. In my mind, it's more important than almost anything else. There comes a point where money just isn't so important. Of course, you have to first get to that point — I understand this, and I worked hard to get to the point where my income is enough so I could start enjoying some time off.

Remember something: Unlike in a job, when you own the business, time off is *not* something you *get* — it's something you have to *take*.

It's the entrepreneur's curse to work a ton of hours. In my opinion, it's not healthy. But again, I fell into this trap — in the beginning, all I did was work. Work for clients, work on my business, work, work, work …

And it's odd, because whenever I was employed, I couldn't stand those guys who worked 80 hours a week and considered you "weak" if you went home after 8 hours a day. They'd say things like "half day?" when I left at 5:00. I usually answered, "No — sane mind." I also hated overtime. Yeah, the money was nice sometimes, but at many of my old jobs, it was seldom optional.

I recall one brief job I had working in a warehouse. It was my job to "pick and pack." I got a list from a guy behind a metal screen and I had to zip around the warehouse on a motorized pallet jack, get the items, and load them onto a truck. Basically, I was paid to go shopping. But the oddest part of this job was the loudspeaker. The loudspeaker was essentially like a booming voice from the heavens. Every so often it would emit a loud BUZZZ, which meant break time. One buzz, and everyone would stop and go to the break room. Another buzz, and everyone went back to work. Now that I think about it, they treated us like lab rats, really.

Anyway, the worst part was when the voice would come on about half an hour before our shift ended and say, "There will be two hours of mandatory overtime." A booming voice from above, telling us we had to stay. Every time that voice came on, all 150 men groaned as if they had been shot. I suspect the guy behind the screen was the voice (hence the need for a metal screen).

The point is, I despised overtime in my jobs, yet here I was in my own business, working every day, week after week after week. Yes, in the beginning, it's necessary to work long hours. And at times, it will become necessary again. (Writing this book is a great example — although I did lighten my schedule for writing it, I still had *some* client work to do. I wrote every single day for several months to get this book done.) And I suspect I'll be putting in some extra hours when I write the pages for a second website I am launching.

However, I have learned when to stop. I suggest you pay attention to this as well. As far as days off, start with one day a week, all major holidays, and two long weekends for the year. Then, as business permits, slowly add to that. During the days you work, work as many hours as you wish, but take the days off I suggest — you'll be happy you did.

Chapter 47

KEEP YOUR MARKETING SIMPLE

One of the biggest movie franchises of all time, if not *the* biggest, is *Star Wars*. While at this writing the tale encompasses six films, it all began with the original — *Star Wars*. And if you were a kid in 1977, you remember just how big *Star Wars* was. Basically, *Star Wars* was *the* biggest event of my first 12 years on the planet. It's essentially all we kids talked about for an entire year, and multiple viewings were not uncommon at all — in fact, they were required by an unspoken law for boys (I saw it six times in 1977).

And while the special effects were really good, we all were enthralled by the story as well. Which, now that I think about it, could have not been more stereotypical.

Follow me here for a second and see just how absurdly basic this movie's plot is. In *Star Wars*, we have —

- a good guy in white,

- a bad guy in black,

- a roguish antihero with his tough sidekick,

- a wise old warrior coming back for one final fight,

- a plucky rebellion going up against a powerful, evil empire,

- a villain's deadly castle (well, space station in this case), and

- comic relief from the robots (or droids).

It's all here. In fact, the only additional plot element we need to go *completely* over the top is a captured princess ... Oh, wait ...

Star Wars works because it's simple good versus evil. Tried and true.

There's a reason the tried and true *is* the tried and true — it works. It should be the same with your marketing, especially in the beginning.

But Wait — What *Is* Marketing?

You'd better pull up a chair before you ask a marketing professional what he or she does for a living, because you're going to be there a while.

I've worked several corporate-type jobs. At most of them, the head of marketing was someone who had been around a while and was a friend of the owner/president. From my observation, it seems nobody rises up through the ranks of the marketing department to be the head of marketing — he or she is simply placed there. In every corporate job I ever had, I never really figured out what the marketing manager did on a day-to-day basis. In corporate America, the marketing department seems like a good place to hide. That's why I always wanted to be a part of it.

In all seriousness, here's how *I* define marketing: Marketing describes *all* of your efforts in trying to get business.

Your advertising is part of your marketing. Your business card is part of your marketing. Your sales calls are part of your marketing. Deciding who will use your product or service is part of your marketing.

It's really that simple — if it in any way will (hopefully) result in business, it's marketing.

Let me explain why I simplify it so (and why I used the oh-so-clever *Star Wars* story): because the word *marketing* is often intimidating to a home-based business owner. Business books and consultants talk about your "marketing plan," or worse yet, your "marketing strategy."

Let's stay away from terms like this for now. We can worry about "marketing strategies" when your business is well beyond the start-up phase. For now, however, let's keep your marketing efforts simple.

Keeping Things Simple

The message for this chapter: Just keep your marketing simple.

I remind you of this because many beginning entrepreneurs want to set the world on fire. They want to use the Internet, get some "viral marketing" going, advertise in odd places, and generally do new or unusual things. Terms like "guerrilla marketing" have become in vogue.

While I won't disagree that a little creativity can be good, for your home-based business in the beginning phases, let's stick to tried and true marketing. This means if you're a plumber, get some business cards made, paint your name on your van, and buy a Yellow Pages ad. If you're starting a website design business, get a website going, hand out flyers to local businesses, and start doing some pay-per-click advertising. Tried and true.

If you want to experiment with odd or new ways of drumming up business, by all means, do so. I encourage it, in fact. But do so *after* you have done the tried and true, and not at their expense. The tried and true are what will get you going. The more oddball things may pay off big, but they can also do absolutely zero. It's too big a risk for a start-up to rely solely on odd or offbeat advertising or marketing methods.

Chapter 48

YOUR COMPETITION

I never really thought much about competition until one night years ago at a Chamber of Commerce function. I was chatting with a tree care professional, and he was talking about his competition. In a word, he was *obsessed* with his competition, and he *hated* them.

So I asked him how business was. He stated it was great — in fact, he had never been busier, and he had to turn down work. So then I asked, "Well, why are you obsessed with your competition? I mean, how many *more* trees can you possibly cut?"

If, as a beginning entrepreneur, you fear and loathe your competition, relax — such thoughts are perfectly normal. However, by and large, your competition is not your enemy to be scorned (or done away with). I look at it more like your competition is a constant but friendly rival. In fact, your competition is necessary and can be a valuable resource for you.

Let's look at some aspects of your competition.

You Can Learn from Your Competition

If your competition is successful, you can learn a lot by studying how they do business. And how do you find out? Well, to begin, you can ask them. It's not unethical or as uncomfortable as you think. Yes, they probably aren't going to open the vault for you, but you'd be surprised what you can learn over a drink at the next Chamber of

Commerce mixer. Introduce yourself to your competition and get acquainted.

In addition, you can shop the competition — relax, everyone does it. Or you can have a friend call them and report back to you. How they answer the phone, what their quote sheet looks like, how they conduct themselves. Trust me; you'll be "shopped" yourself. It's like football teams stealing mascots before the big game.

Your Competition Can Refer Business to You

Your home-based business simply cannot handle everyone who needs your service. There isn't enough time in the day. When I am booked and someone needs something fast, I refer them to competitors. The competitors do the same for me — it all pretty much evens out in the end. I've scored some big contracts this way, and I've given away my share too. Plus, in the end, the client is happy. If the client called me, and I referred them to someone else, and that someone else does a nice job, it's a big feather in my client's cap, but it's also a small feather in mine. I'll take the small feather over no feather at all (if you can't do the work, the client will find a competitor *anyway*). Things like this tend to come back to you in a good way.

You Need Your Competition

Competition forces businesses to stay on their toes and improve themselves. Competition also helps create a market for your services. For example, if you have a competitor that advertises heavily, you will almost certainly benefit from it, as you'll siphon off some overflow business (or people that just weren't satisfied with their service/offer/terms/whatever).

Criticizing Your Competition Is Unprofessional

Even if you have a competitor you don't like, do not criticize them to clients or potential clients. It's not looked upon favorably, and it is not professional. Plus, it will *always* get back to them. It's okay to point out your strong points, but not at anyone else's expense. Lay your cards on the table, and trust that your client is smart enough to figure out who is better.

I try to look at competition more as "we're all in the same boat." And trust me, if one of your competitors goes out of business, someone will fill the void almost right away. If anything, you'll get more competition. I say embrace that fact — there's enough work for everyone.

Chapter 49

NETWORKING, LOCAL ORGANIZATIONS, ETC.

I knew I was in trouble the minute I saw the shiny tin trays with cans of sterno burning underneath. Nothing says mediocre quite like scrambled eggs cooked two hours ago and kept warm by a can of burning gel. Still, I was told this local breakfast networking meeting was a good thing, so I loaded up on bacon, picked out one of the incredibly tough pancakes, and took my seat at the big round table.

Yes, I had joined the Stale Breakfast Club, and I was there to network.

Networking is simply getting yourself out there, shaking hands, handing out your business card, or even just saying hello to someone and talking about business. Networking can be done anywhere — at organized local business organizations, at the local bowling alley, at the convenience store, or even online. Simply meeting someone and exchanging "what do you do you for a living?" information can lead to new clients. In my first business, I got several clients just by saying, "I'm in direct-mail advertising," to someone I met. (I also had people leave right away; while it might be okay for business, it's a terrible pickup line at the bar.)

Before I get into the specifics of networking organizations, let me state that it goes without saying that you should *always* carry business cards and be ready to talk business. Even when you're pumping gas, the guy pumping gas next to you could be a potential client. While I don't recommend just walking up to strangers at the gas station and talking business, if a conversation *does* start, well, just be ready to hand out a business card.

Now let's look at some other networking organizations and situations.

Your Local Chamber of Commerce

Your local Chamber of Commerce is not only a useful resource for networking and meeting other business professionals in your area, it also has its hand on the pulse of local business affairs.

Through the Chamber, you can learn which businesses are coming to the area, what's happening with local establishments, what local zoning changes are upcoming, etc. This is because everyone who is someone in your local area belongs to the Chamber of Commerce. And yes, it is very useful to home-based businesses. The Chamber welcomes all business types and sizes, and can really help your business be seen as a "real" entity. All else being equal, I'd view a Chamber member as more of a "real" business over someone who is not a member. It has nothing to do with being in a clique (there are so many members, it's tough to know them all), and everything to do with professionalism.

Chamber of Commerce membership fees vary depending on your area. I do recommend you join — if not right away, then as soon as you make a little money. Some areas even have more than one Chamber (maybe one for the county/region and one for the town). It doesn't hurt to join both. You need not attend every mixer or function, but Chamber membership opens a lot of doors.

In addition, many Chambers of Commerce offer special benefits to members, such as reduced rates for health insurance, which can easily make a membership pay for itself.

The Rotary Club, Lions Club, Etc.

I have only attended these club meetings as a guest, but I have to say that I found them to be filled with friendly, interesting professionals — the kind of people it never hurts to know on a first-name basis. I don't have the time to join these local clubs at this juncture, but if I were going to join another organization, I'd probably target these. There are worse ways to spend an afternoon a week.

Tip/Lead Clubs and Related Organizations

Tip/lead clubs usually accept only one member from each type of business, and they exchange business leads at meetings. The general premise is that if you know someone who needs a carpenter, and there's a carpenter in your tip club, that carpenter gets the lead.

Truth be told, I don't like any type of club and/or organization that "strongly" encourages you to do business with (and to give leads to) other members. Any club that "forces" you to give leads, or limits membership to one of each business type, is not very professional, and not a place I recommend you spend your time. The stale breakfast club I mentioned earlier actually fined you a dollar if you didn't provide a lead for someone else in the club at every meeting. Like the threat of losing a dollar would be enough to persuade me to recommend Blowtorch Al's Body Shop to a loved one who just had a fender bender. Um, no thanks.

I joined a few such organizations as a young, naïve businessman. However, I soon found out they consisted mostly of fringe, sales-oriented businesspeople: your new-to-the-business cut-rate financial planner was there, hustling for leads; the local network marketing dreamer was there, looking to offer people "the opportunity" to sell all-natural seaweed jelly; and the worst body shop in town was represented by a rather greasy man who always seemed to sit next to me.

I learned to avoid these types of clubs/meetings. Not only was the food terrible, the forced-lead policy pretty much ensured lousy leads. (I recall several times saying, "Hi, Joe sent me," only to be asked, "Who's Joe?" which leads to a fairly awkward business moment.) But, if you enjoy getting up early, eating chewy pancakes, and recommending businesses for no other reason than to save a dollar, these clubs might be right up your alley.

Online Networking

Online networking is primarily done through online message forums or groups. If you don't know what I'm talking about, go to any search engine and type in "[*your business type*] forum" and look through the results. Chances are you will come across numerous discussion forums or message boards pertaining to your business. If you find one (or several) that interest you, join the group and join the discussions.

I cannot say enough about online networking. Not only are online message forums a great place to connect with colleagues and bounce ideas off people in your specific business, they gave my current business its start, as I will explain shortly.

So start posting on forums. Include a link to your website in all of your posts. You never know where it will lead.

The Other Uses of Online Message Forums

In addition to possibly getting business, online message forums are exceptional for *providing* information. It is somewhere you can connect with other professionals in your line of work. And because most participants in online forums do not directly compete with you due to geographical location, they are *much* more open in terms of sharing information. Want to know what other professionals in your line of work charge? How they screen out trouble clients? What advertising worked for them? Join an online message forum for your type of business and start participating. You'll get your answers.

There's a message forum for just about every conceivable profession or topic. There are forums for exterminators, web designers, photographers, beekeepers, mushroom growers, alpaca breeders, beer brewers, and just about anything else.

I like to use the word *slug* when I'm joking around, so for fun, I searched for "slug forum" — would you know I found one for sea slugs? Did you even know there *were* sea slugs? I didn't. Apparently not only are there sea slugs, but people actually want to talk about them.

Online forums are useful, plentiful, and best of all, free. Join up, and start participating. You'll soon find out that online message forums are one of the best resources available to you.

The Better Business Bureau

While not really a networking organization, I'd like to take a moment to mention the Better Business Bureau.

The Better Business Bureau (BBB) is misunderstood by many people. It is not an official government organization, and it wields very little (if any) power over nonmembers.

Businesses join the BBB voluntarily. The businesses that *do* join are interested in keeping their good name with the BBB. But there's little the BBB can do to a nonmember business. Saying to a nonmember business, "I'm going to contact the Better Business Bureau" is about as effective as saying, "I'm going to tell my mom on you."

In fact, depending on whose mom we're talking about, the mom thing might be *more* effective.

Upon joining the BBB, a business essentially pledges to do business in an ethical manner, and agrees to resolve disputes in a certain fashion. Consumers complaining about a member business can cause the business to have its membership revoked.

The BBB's revenue largely comes from the yearly fees that member businesses pay. It's been called a "paid seal of approval" by critics — in other words, you paid to be a member, and you weren't chosen because your business is good.

That being said, I am personally a member, and I have found it useful. Being able to display the BBB seal on my website has made people feel good about doing business with me. It basically proves that I pledge to do business a certain way. I'm absolutely certain that it has helped my business. I like being a BBB member, and I do recommend it.

DAN'S STORY: FROM ONLINE NETWORKING TO SELF-EMPLOYMENT

Years ago, I was working for a pocketknife company. I was hired to do e-commerce programming for them. To this day, I don't understand why I got hired, because I didn't have any e-commerce *or* programming experience. I guess they just wanted someone who was good with a computer in an overall way. Regardless, I got hired, and set about learning how to do the programming they needed.

The software they needed me to operate was for a specific task. Orders would come in over the computers in a specific language used for commerce (this is how almost all big companies communicate with each other), and the specific software I used would translate these electronic orders into something my company's computer system could understand (the software made "data maps" that translated the data).

(continued)

It took me about six months, but I became an expert with this software. In fact, I became so good at it, I kind of worked myself out of a job. I had hours a day where I literally had nothing to do. So these hours were filled with pretend work. Like, communicating with people on online forums and message boards. I was on forums for games. I was on discussion groups for my favorite sports teams, and I also was a regular on a forum for this specific piece of e-commerce translation software I used.

My time on the software forum was spent basically answering other people's questions. Anyone reading the forum would conclude that I was an expert on the software because of the volume of questions I answered. So one day, a consultant in Florida was surfing the web, looking for someone to use this software to make translation maps for one of his clients. He found the forum and saw that I was the guy answering questions. He emailed me and asked if I could help him. I figured, what the heck — I had my own copy of the translation software at home, so why not?

In essence, I would be doing the exact same job for the Florida Company as I did for the pocketknife company I worked for. Except instead of a salary, I'd charge an hourly consultant rate, and instead of an office on-site, I'd do the work at my home and email them the data maps.

Anyway, the very day after hearing from the Florida people, I got into an argument with my boss, and was fired. Seems my hours of pretend work were not enough to keep me around. This wasn't bad, however — it really set things in motion, because this company in Florida actually had a *lot* of work for me. When I started doing work for them on a consultant/freelance basis, I figured there must be other companies out there looking for the same thing. I learned years ago not to put all my eggs in one basket, so I made myself a website offering my e-commerce mapmaking skills. I advertised online, put my website link in my messages on forums, and emailed companies that used this specific software. Within a few days, I started getting email from other companies. Nothing big (this wasn't popular software), but I added about a client a month.

That very first year, I earned more than I would have at the pocketknife company, and even outearned the boss who fired me. Let me tell you, at that time, there was nothing sweeter than knowing that fact. I still owe her a thank-you card. The programming eventually gave way to writing, but that's how my current business actually started.

All of this is a direct result of networking online.

Chapter 50

BE PATIENT, BUT BE READY FOR CHANGE, TOO

This chapter is a quick reminder of something that is often forgotten — the importance of patience.

One of the great things about entrepreneurs is that we are full of ideas. One of the bad things about entrepreneurs is that we are full of ideas.

That's not a misprint — this is a true double-edged sword.

By our very nature, entrepreneurs like to try things, and are always looking for the next big idea. We are a very eager bunch. This can be detrimental to your home-based business. I have seen far too many entrepreneurs become impatient when they don't make money right away — and they change the focus of their business.

Heck, I was one of them. After my direct-mail enterprise wasn't making enough (due to my numerous mistakes and my need for immediate income), I switched gears to selling ad space on videotape rental boxes. (A great idea, really — I provided video stores with cases that had local ads on them. I gave them the case free, and I also paid a dollar a case for them to carry it.) When I botched the video rental case thing, I switched to selling T-shirts with slogans on them. When that wasn't going so well, I switched to selling pens and other ad specialty items.

And all the while, I was doing graphic design and other advertising-type work. All this within two years. In short, I didn't give anything even a scant chance. I switched gears right away. The direct mail, since I began with it, lasted the longest. But after that, it seemed like every month I was doing something different.

This is the kiss of death. You simply cannot wear so many hats. I had to learn the hard way. When clients see you changing focus every few months, they wonder what's going on. Short-term change is not a good thing.

So my advice is to avoid doing this. Stick to the business you start. Branch out to other things after you have succeeded with the first one, or after you have given it a fair chance. In other words, if you're a plumber, be a plumber. If you can at all help it, don't take jobs doing roofing unless you want to expand to a general contracting business. Scattershot work may pay the bills in the short term, but it is always a bad idea in the long term, because you lose focus on your business and start living week to week, taking whatever work you can get. It won't be long before you're doing something *way* out of your realm. I know contractors who started mowing lawns — there's nothing wrong with mowing lawns, mind you (many landscaping services do well) — but you're not going to build your contracting business that way.

One big reason one ends up adopting this scattershot approach to work is because people start businesses needing immediate income. As I already mentioned earlier in the book, this is not a smart idea, and should be avoided at all costs. If money is *that* tight, you're probably better off going back to regular full-time employment than working all these jobs in an attempt to become self-employed.

Now, Be Ready to Change

Take a look at your local Main Street or shopping district. Does it look the same as it did 10 or 15 years ago? Chances are, it doesn't. (For one thing, I noticed there are a lot more karate studios these days — when did that happen? They all have similar phone numbers, too: 555-KICK or 555-CHOP.)

Main Street is different than it used to be because business never stays the same. So right after telling you to be patient, I am going to tell you to keep change in the back of your mind. Not little changes to help pay this month's mortgage, but big changes that will affect the overall course of your business.

Getting a full-blown website is a change like this. Offering a new service or product line is a change like this. For myself, I will soon be launching a new website that will focus more on the corporate market.

Just keep in mind that ten years from now, your business will probably not be like it is today. Change is inevitable. Embrace it when you feel the time is right. How will you know when the time is right? Simple: when you're doing well enough that there's consistent money left over at the end of the month. Money that should go back into your business. But these advanced problems are for another book.

Chapter 51

EVERYBODY SAYS THEY CARE ABOUT CUSTOMERS. BUT DO YOU? REALLY?

I talk to businesspeople all the time, and you would be stunned by how scornful many of them are toward customers.

And you know what's really surprising? That this is more common among small businesses than large. It's something you will probably have to guard against.

Listen, there are some customers who simply need more attention than others. Unless it truly becomes unreasonable, this is nothing more than a part of doing business — you can't let it upset you. These types of customers are simply customers — they are not "annoying customers." Okay, wait, maybe they are … But you can't let them know that by your actions. Breathe that heavy sigh *after* you get off the phone with them.

Also, some customers will "price shop." Again, you should expect this — that's part of being in business. You may drive a half hour to bid on a job and end up losing it to your competitor because he or she quoted $50 less. That doesn't mean the customer is a "cheap @#$%." It simply means they saw more value in saving $50 than they saw in your superior work. You should thank this customer instead. He or she demonstrated that you need to improve on pointing out the value of your work, and justifying your price.

I truly like almost all of my clients and potential clients — even the ones I do not end up doing business with. True, there are some who waste my time and are simply looking for the cheapest deal, and there are some who are harder to deal with than others, but these are such a minority that it's not even worth discussing.

Every customer — every single one — is an opportunity to improve your business.

Chapter 52

CUTTING TIES: SOME CLIENTS JUST AREN'T WORTH IT

Here's the flip side to my "every customer is an opportunity to improve your business" speech.

Okay, every customer *is* an opportunity to improve your business. Just a tiny number of those customers allow us to improve by showing us just how much to tolerate before saying "enough" and pulling out a baseball bat. Hey, learning when to say "enough" is an improvement. Technically, anyway. So is practicing your baseball swing.

Learning when to say "enough" is not really difficult. You say it to a client when interacting with them starts to affect you above and beyond the work you are doing for them. For example, if there's a knot in your stomach every time you deal with a client, it might be best to cut ties.

Don't fall into the trap of "the customer is always right." While nobody works harder to please clients than I do, that statement gets more businesses in trouble than any other. Simply put, the customer is sometimes wrong. Dead wrong. And you should not suffer because of it.

Here are some good examples of when you may want to cut ties:

- When a client gives you excess stress or mental strain.

- When a client becomes abusive or yells.

- When a client's expectations are unrealistic, despite your best efforts to point out the extent and limit of your work.

- When payment becomes an issue. Once a second invoice is late, action must be taken.

Cutting Ties

There's a nice way to cut ties. Under no circumstances should you burn bridges. Even if someone owes you a lot of money, don't burn the bridge. Just say that no more work will be done until payment is received. If they come back to you a year later for more work, present the old invoice (trust me, they haven't forgotten, and neither should you). If you left the relationship somewhat neutral or amicable, you just may collect, and win back the business.

Also, if you cut ties for whatever reason, you owe the customer a refund for unused funds. In fact, if possible, refund the complete deposit. (Obviously, if you bought materials that you can't reuse, or already did work, this won't apply.) Pay them promptly, without being asked. This is professional, and it goes a *long* way in keeping a relationship at least amicable.

I have had an occasional issue or two with clients. One was *very* upset with what I wrote, and another presented me with a job I felt I just couldn't write, because I knew that the business model would not work. When I cut ties with each of them, I **immediately** refunded their money. The problems and bad feelings that keeping their money would have brought were simply not worth it. In fact, I later ended up doing more work for one of them, which never would have happened if I had not given them a prompt refund.

It basically comes down to this: Cutting ties in an amicable, professional manner will never hurt you.

Stop the Madness Before It Even Starts

I'm not one to prejudge clients. I learned from selling cars years ago not to prejudge anyone. Often the worst-dressed people had the most money and the best credit rating. However, there are times when I can just "tell" a client is going to be trouble. Here are my four warning signs:

1. They string you along. Lots of promises, but no money. To combat this, I stop chasing fairly quickly into the relationship.

2. A million phone calls or questions before the project has even begun. I don't mind a reasonable amount of questions or phone calls, but at some point, I have to say "enough."

3. Any type of overly "stern" or unrealistically speculative behavior on their part. I tend to get a little wary if I hear statements like, "Okay, now I'm going to get my writing next week, riiiight?? And it's going to make the customers beat down my door, CORRECT?"

4. Prospective clients who really didn't like my price but say something like, "Okay, you'd *better* be worth it." While I've had a few of these who were happy with my work, I had a few others that there was just no pleasing.

I'm not saying these warning signs will make me not accept the client. But building a fair and reasonable "overly difficult client fee" invisibly into my price makes it easier. And, it also makes the really difficult ones go away.

Chapter 53

MAKE SURE YOU TAKE TIME TO WORK *ON* YOUR BUSINESS

It might seem odd that I have to remind people about this, but it is *very* easy to get so caught up in doing the day-to-day work for clients that you forget you are actually running a business.

I know people that do *nothing* but work for months straight; then, when the slower times come, they have no clients because they totally let their marketing/advertising slip. Or they get so caught up in clients' projects that they have no time to organize their office and make sure their invoicing is current. It's the old "everybody in town has nice shoes except the cobbler's kids."

Here's how you combat this: For one day a month, you work solely *on* your business, not *in* it. You will likely need to schedule this — may I suggest a Friday, which is probably the easiest on your schedule.

I cannot stress how important working *on* your business is. In fact, I feel it's so important that I do it *twice* a month instead of just once. I literally have two "work days" a month where I do nothing but check my advertising, add pages to my website, make sure my billing and invoicing are current, make sure there are no leftover issues, explore new ways to market, research new website tools like pop-ups and forms, etc.

I don't schedule client work for these days, and I answer email sparingly. Of course, I always have the option to help a client in an emergency if need be, but by and large, these days are for working *on* the business.

While it's true I bring in no direct money on these days in the form of billing, they are *by far* the most profitable days I work. I fine-tune my online ads, think up new ways to sell my services, target new prospective clients, write introduction letters, come up with a new product or service to offer — the list goes on and on.

So you should be doing this at least one day a month. If your schedule is such that you cannot, then you are going to have to take a Saturday or another scheduled day off. Yes, it is *that* important.

Taking a day or two a month to work *on* your business also serves as a constant reminder that you are *in business*. All too often, people starting a business end up with a "job" where they are the owner. Entire books have been written on this very subject — I'm covering it here in a page or two, but the overall message is the same: Take time to work *on* your business. It's the only way it will really grow.

Putting Money Back

There's another aspect to this: Money needs to go back into your business. You have to treat your business like a living, breathing entity, and it needs to be taken care of.

A lot of home-based business owners forget this, and think the business is just there to provide them with income. This is because many home-based businesses start with the idea of providing a full-time income fairly quickly. And there is nothing wrong with expecting a full-time income within a reasonable time frame (although expecting that right away, as I mentioned earlier, is not the best thing). However, do not let yourself get caught up in "I work five or six days per week and the money I make pays the bills." That's a slow, steady road to oblivion. The reality is the business will slowly die without a steady diet of money. You must expand; you can't be stagnant. In business, being stagnant is the same as regressing.

This doesn't mean you have to expand in the classic sense. Just computerizing your billing, for example, can be considered "expansion." Or upgrading to a better vehicle if you're a tradesperson. Or investing in a new, better website.

But regardless of how you expand and grow, the fact remains that you *must* expand. Because if you don't, your competition will blow right past you. I see it happening now — old-time contractors losing business to a contractor with a website and who can answer email. Or people with websites made five years ago (a lifetime in Internet years) still trying to do business today. Or people still answering the phone with "Hello" and wondering why business is slow …

The list goes on and on.

There is no formula for how much money should go back into your business. It depends on your personal needs, your business needs, and your situation in life. But please understand that *something* must go back. Because without some type of growth or expansion, your business will slowly regress.

Chapter 54

THE OTHER SIDE OF THE COIN — BEING A GOOD CUSTOMER

"Treat people the way you'd want to be treated."

We've heard this line since grade school, but it doesn't seem to be exercised at all times. For example, it seems to get lost on me when I'm behind the wheel of a car, or, say, when a fast-food clerk hands me a mayonnaise-laden Drippy Burger when I *clearly* said "no mayo."

However, this really isn't about clerks, cashiers, or other drivers ... No, I'm talking about being a good client in business-to-business relationships.

I've noticed something during my years in business: While many of us *want* good clients and customers, we're not such good clients and customers *ourselves*.

Someone once complained to me that he hated it when people tried to negotiate his price. He said he was worth the money, and his customers should see that. He wanted me to write his literature pointing that out.

He then immediately proceeded to negotiate *my* price. And he was *very* difficult about it. Suffice to say, he never became my client.

Be Someone People *Want* to Do Business With

I feel a key to success is not only providing great service to others, but also being someone others want to provide great service *to*.

I am absolutely convinced that if you are a great client — if you're a person or company that others like doing business with — it will only help you in your business efforts. After all, part of running a good business is making sure others will do great work for you when needed. And the best way to ensure that is being someone others *want* to do business with.

I've developed some rules for being a good client, and I can say in all honesty that I practice these myself. I am just as proud when someone tells me I'm a great client as I am when someone tells me I'm a great writer.

Here are some rules I suggest you try to follow:

- Most professionals charge a fair rate for their services, so if you want *their* service, pay *their* rate. If someone else will do the work for less, by all means go to someone else if cost is your leading criterion. But don't ask Peter to match Paul's rate if you truly want Peter's work.

- Pay your bills on time. I pay bills as soon as I get them. People *love* that. It makes other businesses want to do business with me. I know that clients who pay me on time, all the time, get better attention from me. That's just a fact of business.

- When you hire someone, don't assume what's an easy job and what isn't. The bottom line for me is, if I can't do the same work myself, I have no basis to assume something is easy or quick. Saying, "This should be a simple job ..." to a professional is somewhat dismissive of his or her skill and talent. It's almost like you're

saying, "Hey, I can do this *easily*, but I choose not to."

- It's probably okay to act that way when you hire a kid to mow your lawn. Heck, you *know* how easy or hard that is. But don't say that to professionals. Sometimes, a seemingly simple job isn't so simple.

- Don't be pushy. My email messages simply have a link to my website. If I see you in person, perhaps I'll hand you a business card. And that's about the extent of my pushing my services. Everyone who does work for me knows what I do for a living, and I'd welcome them to use my services if the need arises. But I do not *expect* a reciprocating business relationship, and won't push for one.

- Realize that the people who work for you are human. They get sick. They have occasional emergencies. They have to go to unexpected funerals. Good clients understand this, so be understanding of the people who work for you.

- At the same time, be as attentive to people working for you as you are to your own clients. You need to follow through on everything. If you told them you'd give them information next week so they can do the job, get them the information they need next week. Even if something arises, a phone call can make all the difference. Yes, you may be really busy, but so are the people who do work for you.

The key thing to remember is to be a good client yourself. Your business will only be stronger because of it.

Chapter 55

SOME FINAL THOUGHTS

I pondered and pondered how to end the section I chose to call Soul, and how to end this entire book. Then I realized there were a few final, somewhat random points that I still wanted to go over (or things I mentioned earlier and wanted to expand on), so this seemed the perfect place to put them.

You Will Experience the Highest of Highs, and the Lowest of Lows

The day you sign that big client, or make that first big sale, or sign that contract ... oh, is that a great day! I remember when I got my first "good sized" project. I was going to earn in three months what it took me a year to earn at some of my previous jobs. My wife and I went out to dinner to celebrate — it felt awesome. There is no rosier outlook than the day you sign a decent-size client, or make a big sale. It *never* gets old.

On the flip side, there's going to be a day when a steady client drops you. Or something changes and all of a sudden you're faced with a big drop in your income. Or a four-figure check bounces, and you hear all kinds of talk from the client except the one thing you want to hear: "Here's the money." Not only does it seem like the check will never be made good, but you realize you're going to lose future business that you counted on ... and the holidays are coming. This has happened to me, and it's a dark day indeed.

The important part to remember is to keep an even, steady manner. Yes, go out to dinner when you get a big client. Be happy and celebrate. And yes, get angry or depressed the day a bad thing happens.

Then get up the next morning and conduct business as usual.

Spend Wisely

Given that both ups and downs happen, it is important not to base your expenses/purchases on one day's business. Getting a big client does *not* mean you should run right out and buy a new car. Far too many people do just that (or something similar). It's a silly move, because you never know what's going to happen. Nothing is guaranteed. Your new customer could have a fire and be out of business in a month, and you're holding a $75,000 note on a new Jaguar. This kind of stuff happens to people. They'll bemoan their bad luck and terrible break, but the truth is, situations like this were completely preventable.

A better thing to do is wait until you have several years of good growth, solid funds in the bank, and a full work schedule for the foreseeable future. Then it's okay to go car shopping.

In Business, Money Means Everything

I know I already alluded to this earlier, but it's important. When you get down to the real nitty gritty, money counts, and everything else is meaningless.

Promises are meaningless. Handshakes are meaningless. Even making a sale is meaningless until you actually get paid for it. Money talks — everything else is BS. Even contracts are meaningless — contracts are only worthwhile if you are willing to go to court to enforce them. Otherwise, a contract is a worthless piece of paper. And you probably already know a check is worthless until it clears.

If you have a promise, or a contract, or a signature, or a handshake agreement, you have nothing until you actually get paid. Please don't ever forget that.

Just About All Business Relationships End

I alluded to this earlier in the 80/20 rule, but it's worth repeating here. While I take great care to be someone people want to do business with, I am always aware of one simple fact — almost all business relationships end at some point.

This isn't being pessimistic or a paranoid statement — it's just a simple fact. Be it by your choice, their choice, the whims of fate, a new partner, a new operations manager, fires, floods, earthquakes, bankruptcy, change in direction, a boss's child taking over, swarms of locusts eating the crops of your biggest client … whatever. All business relationships eventually end. It could take one year, five years, ten years, or more. It could be sudden, or it could be a gradual drop-off. You may see it coming, or it may blindside you.

Nobody and no business is immune to this. Even today's biggest companies will eventually go out of business or get bought or completely change. It's inevitable.

While losing a big client or major supplier can hurt, as long as you keep this in mind and are somewhat prepared for it, it won't hurt as much.

You Will Never, Ever Be Completely Comfortable — So Relax, It's Normal

I have a successful writing business. I have a nice website that gets a lot of traffic. I often have to turn away work. Heck, I'm even writing a book! You'd think I've made it, right?

Then why am I always nervous about business? Why am I always thinking the end is right around the corner?

I'm not alone. My brother-in-law owns a successful jewelry store. In business more than ten years, his store services thousands of customers. By all accounts, he's made it. Yet still, to this day, he thinks that every customer walking through that door is the last one — *ever*. In his mind, there will be no more customers.

My other brother-in-law owns a painting business. He feels like each job is his last one. It doesn't matter how far out he's booked — the wolf is always at the door in his mind.

In talking with entrepreneurs from all walks of life, this feeling is very common. In fact, I have yet to meet a successful entrepreneur who doesn't feel this way. Even millionaires who built huge companies never lose that anxious feeling.

It is almost certain that you will feel the same way. You will always be anxious in terms of business, no matter how successful you are. It's okay — it's normal. It comes from the same place that gives us our inner drive and fire. Without this feeling of anxiousness, we'd be satisfied with working a regular job.

It's part of being an entrepreneur. Embrace it.

And with that incredibly nice line, I'll come to the end of this book. Although I wrote most of the book out of order (many chapters sprang up from nothing as I realized there was something else I wanted to discuss), this is really the last part (apart from the afterword) that I'm writing. It feels somewhat odd — almost 80,000 words, and here I am at the end. I'd be lying if I didn't say I was a little sad.

I truly hope this book has helped you. I figure if I got you to think a little bit, and perhaps got you to implement just *one* suggestion from the book, then I'm happy. I'd love it if you followed every piece of advice I gave, but I know that's impractical. But again, I really hope you got something useful out of it. Everything written here — every word, strategy, and piece of advice, is meant to help you succeed.

I feel so very fortunate to be as successful in business as I have been, and I want you to feel the same way.

Afterword

WHY I'M AN ENTREPRENEUR (OR, "WORK IS A FOUR-LETTER WORD")

I have always been what my wife calls "unemployable." In fact, I've gone through more jobs in one week (three) than my wife has gone through in her entire life. I have had over 20 jobs in my life, and never lasted more than a few years at any single job (and sometimes I only lasted a few hours).

However, I'm a good writer, I've always been aggressive, and I do well at interviews, so I was always able to land on my feet whenever I was "let go." Only to be let go again two years later. Bosses seem to get tired of me after two years.

I guess I have to admit it — I am a bad employee. I just never understood the arbitrary rules that many jobs seem to have that nobody could really explain to me. For example, I can see why at certain jobs you

have to start at a certain time. Shifts and hours of operation (like at a retail store) dictate rigid work hours. I get that. But I have worked plenty of jobs that involved office-type work that really didn't *require* me showing up at a specific time. Does a programmer, a graphic artist, or a book editor *really* have to be there at 9 a.m.? Why not 10 a.m.? Or 10:30, and stay until 7:00?

I posed this question to several of my (many) employers. I never once received an honest, logical answer. I was always told something stupid like, "That's the way it is." Yeah, good answer.

Now, I understand some basic reasons why I just can't make my own hours arbitrarily. Normal business hours are nine to five. If I want to interact with coworkers

195

and peers in other companies, I have to be there for at least some of those hours. I get that. But really, is it essential to doing my job that I show up at 9 a.m.? Or is it more essential to some arbitrary form of control by an insecure management? I'm betting the latter.

The best boss I ever had was a man named Pete. Pete hired me to run a store. Pete told me during my interview, "I don't care when you come in or when you leave. In fact, if things are running well and the store is making money, just show up every Friday for your paycheck." I thrive in an atmosphere like that (and often worked more than 40 hours). I had a good two years there, until Pete's boss got tired of me (and Pete!).

No matter what the job, I always seemed to rebel against arbitrary rules. Nothing as blatant as showing up at 10 a.m. every day, but I had many bouts with the dreaded four-day-weekend "stomach flu." Have you ever had that? It's terrible, isn't it? It's almost as bad as the inventory-day fever blisters or the "overloaded shipping dock means we all have to pitch in and load trucks" head cold. Those are serious illnesses that need immediate attention. I recommend plenty of rest at a place where no coworkers will see you.

After all, you're likely contagious.

That's another thing that used to gall me — the "sick day" thing. You are allowed sick days, but you are frowned upon for taking them. And the boss always wants you to call him or her directly if you're going to call in sick. The heck with that — I leave a voice mail at 1 a.m. This is because I will be *far too sick* to get up in the morning and call. It's hard to argue with that logic (the additional benefit is voice mail tends to be very understanding about you calling in sick). Oh, and I'm going to be too sick to answer the phone, too. The fools always tried to call. Like I *might* answer. Imagine that.

Let me illustrate how vicious companies can be in this regard.

At every company there's some jerk who never misses a day. Don't try and compete with this guy — he's an idiot. At one of my jobs, a guy in my department did it *three* years in a row. You know what they gave him? A certificate (unframed) and *five* extra paid vacation days each year. Sounds great, until you realize the company offered 11 sick days per year.

On the other hand, I took all 11 sick days every year. My coworker with perfect attendance was at the company three times longer than I was but I made more money and eventually got promoted over him. After I left, I heard he got cut in the first round of layoffs while people with less tenure who had all sorts of odd ailments kept their jobs. I have one word for him — foolish. He actually thought that being there every day was a positive thing. It wasn't. All he got was an "attaboy." As a final insult, his perfect attendance is never mentioned when people call for references (as human resources is tight-lipped on this stuff).

So follow this logic: I took time off whether ill or not, and the company gave me 11 paid days off per year. My coworker came in when feeling lousy, and they gave him five paid days off. Isn't that bizarre?

Sick days aside, there are other things about my jobs that used to annoy the hell out of me. Like the dress code. Here I was, in an office all day, and they wanted me to play dress-up.

Why?

Why was it important that I wear a tie when the only people who would see me were my coworkers? Couldn't we all just have a meeting and decide once and for all that ties and sports coats were unnecessary? I know many executives swear by a dress code, but I find it arbitrary. Sorry.

Then we have not-so-casual Friday. Wanna see the boss freak out? Wear sweats on casual Friday. You'll be asked to leave (yippee!).

Apparently, casual Friday means Dockers. Gee, what a treat.

But these are all silly gripes. If I had to, I could play the game (except when sick!). That's not the reason I wanted to work for myself. The real reason I work for myself is this: No company, not one, has ever cared one bit about me.

If you've done any reading during the last ten years, the words *downsize* or *outsource* shouldn't give you pause. They are common words these days. Corporations downsized millions of workers and outsourced millions of jobs over the past 15 years. Losing a job disrupts lives, and it disrupts families. It's not a nice thing, no matter who you are. Whether the downsizing or outsourcing is deserved or not, there's one thing almost all downsized workers have in common: When they originally took the job, they did *not* expect to be downsized.

People just don't expect it to happen *to them*. But it does happen, and it will happen to almost everyone at some point. One thing is certain — there's a good chance you will not be at your current job in five years' time. It's even more doubtful you will be there ten years from now.

Whether you work at a corporation, an advertising firm, a private lumberyard, or a car dealership, the odds are overwhelming that you will experience job turnover at some point, either by your choice or theirs. Hopefully yours, but probably theirs.

I'm not here to argue whether or not downsizing is bad. I'm sure companies have their reasons for reducing staff or redirecting resources or restructuring assets or whatever other feel-good term they can think of. My point here is to gently remind you that *your job doesn't care about you*! You are a nameless, faceless cog in the great corporate wheel, and you are also expensive, with those pesky health benefits and 401k contributions.

If it comes down to a choice between you and a reasonable savings, you are *gone*.

History.

Yesterday's news.

If your company thinks, for even one second, that it can both save money and not disrupt things too much by letting you go, you will be out the door before the ink is dry on that report. In business, there is no loyalty.

That is one of the biggest myths about work — that loyalty exists. That the company actually cares about you. Many old-timers still feel that way, and feel some sort of devotion to the company. That devotion is misplaced, however.

Stay at a company long enough, and the odds are overwhelming that it will end badly for you.

Here's a story of a long-term employee whom I watched get the shaft. I was at my first job that really mattered. I was 19 and a salesclerk in a big, family-owned deep-discount department store. This place was huge and, at its prime, employed about 350 people. It was one of those places that sold a little bit of everything at bargain prices, including closeouts and other substandard (a nice word for crappy) merchandise. Hordes of bargain hunters rushed through those doors, sometimes literally knocking us salesclerks over while we were putting out new merchandise. Have you ever been stampeded by four heavyset women all fighting for the one "slightly damaged" bookcase you are putting on the shelf? I have. And I don't recommend it. (As an aside, I also don't recommend "slightly damaged" bookcases, as this was usually code for "ran into it with the forklift.")

The store was owned and run by one man, and his entire family worked there in various important positions. I was known as "Dan from Lumber" (your department was your identity to everyone else in the store). It was a great place for a 19-year-old to work, because it was filled with young, single people like me. I enjoyed working there a lot, and I dated many a pretty cashier (including "Trish from Appliances" and "Dawn from the Front Desk").

Okay, so now I've been there two years, and I get promoted to floor manager. Let me tell you, it was great. I got a desk in an office, I didn't have to punch in anymore (got paid salary instead), and, most importantly, I was transformed from "Dan from Lumber"

into "Dan Furman" when I was paged on the PA (this was actually a very big deal to me at the time). I also got to hire people. (One of my first hires was my brother Russ … I'll never forget giving Russ the tour of the venerable building's second floor. "Okay Russ, don't step there, or you'll fall through.") I really felt proud.

So here I am at this job, loving every minute of it. Things went great for another year or two. I really felt like I belonged and I had this great sense of loyalty. In fact, I even turned down an excellent job at a competing store because I felt "loyalty to the company."

It was now 1988, and the big galleria-type malls were getting built all over. Plus, the big discount chains were coming, and you all know what that meant. Our store just couldn't compete. It had low prices, but it was dirty, inefficient, loud, and generally an unpleasant place to shop. I started to hear rumblings about declining sales and the like. (I wasn't privy to that type of info because I was only a floor manager.)

But my bosses were obviously nervous.

The head manager of the department I worked in (Auto/Home Improvement) had been there for over 20 years. Let's call him "Stan" (so I don't get sued). He had worked his way up from salesclerk many years back and had helped build the place into what it was. The owners loved Stan, and he was considered almost a part of the family. That is, until the sales started to fall.

I'd like to say the owners of the store made some bold decisions in an attempt to compete. That maybe they spent a few bucks to clean the place up and make people want to shop there more. I wish I could say that, but you all know I can't. Instead, I'll tell you what happened: Since my department's sales fell the hardest, Stan was cut loose. I suppose slightly damaged bookcases were not in vogue anymore.

Just like that — 20 years of hard work and loyalty, and he was cut loose without a second thought.

I vividly remember the day it happened: I was talking to him in our shared office when the operations manager stormed in, threw me out, and fired Stan. Stan had suspected it was coming (the day before, he was asked to leave an important meeting), and when it was over he tearfully gathered up 20 years' worth of personal items, put them into a shopping cart, and asked me to let him exit the store through the warehouse door so he wouldn't have to walk through the whole store and have people line the aisles for his death march. It was a very sad moment to witness this man get his very *soul* cut out. Because that's what it was to him. He felt he had given his soul to this place, and they cut him loose without a second thought. One bad quarter, one meeting, and he was gone.

> **And that's my point — in today's world, you (yes, you) are probably one meeting away from pushing your possessions out the door in a shopping cart. Don't think for one minute it is any other way.**

I'm not saying that upper management wasn't justified — maybe he did deserve to be let go (I honestly don't know). But my point is, *he* didn't think so. He felt loyalty to an entity that didn't feel the same loyalty back. They might have given him the *impression* that they would be loyal to him, but in reality, he mattered only to the bottom line. A cold, hard fact of life that we forget all too often.

That day changed me a little bit. I got a little cynical regarding the place, and I also read the writing on the wall. I left for a better job shortly after Stan's demise. After I left, the managers hired a "retail specialist" and he fired even more old-timers (including the operations manager) before running the place into the ground. The store went out of business a few years later. A sad end to a good business.

Who Will Take Care of You?

Think about your job: What would you do without it? Would your family survive? Is it fair to say your life would change dramatically if your main source of income were suddenly taken away from you? Don't think it can't happen — I said before that you are always one meeting away from being unemployed. I meant that. You really are.

Plus, in this post-9/11 world, life (and industry) can change very fast. What would your company do if your biggest customer were the victim of a terrorist attack? Or if your company's product were suddenly blackballed?

In my last "official" job, I worked for one of the world's largest knife manufacturers. After 9/11, pocketknives were no longer allowed in schools or on planes. Parents stopped buying their kids pocketknives. Some large retailers stopped carrying my company's products due to public-relations issues. Know what happened? A big, successful company over 95 years old was put out of business in about three years. Seven hundred jobs — gone.

This can happen to you. I don't care *who* you are or *who* you work for. Even Microsoft can be a memory very quickly in this day and age. Don't think Bill Gates doesn't know that — that's why he still works.

Let's face it; you are hugely reliant on your job. You and your family depend on that weekly paycheck. Most people do not want to think about a time when that check is no longer coming in.

However, *you do have to think about that dark day.*

It's foolish to think your job will provide for anything longer than the short term. The writing is on the wall all around you — ignore the signs at your own peril. A basic premise of capitalism is "make it cheaper." But, in direct contrast to that, we require more and more income as we age. Can you see the conflict?

There was a time when most folks took care of themselves. They either farmed for themselves, worked for another family, worked in a trade, or did *something* that was of value to others. But we've moved away from that. Self-reliance is out. Getting a "good job" is in. It worked great for the first three-quarters of the twentieth century. Unfortunately, we still subscribe to the notion of work taking care of us, even as the old rules get thrown out.

That was me. After I lost my last job at the knife company (fired again!), I was nervous. I didn't know where the money would come from. As mentioned, I did e-commerce (EDI) programming for the knife company, which is a fancy way of saying I dealt with the software that handled orders that came in electronically (almost all large businesses now order products this way). I'm not a highly skilled programmer either. In fact, I have no special computer skills — but I know my way around computers pretty well. So basically, I had no real career skills. I was sunk.

Well, not really … The rest of the story has graced the pages of this book.

The following are included on the enclosed CD-ROM for use on a Windows-based PC. The forms are in PDF and MS Word formats.

Forms

- Your plan for your business
- Start-up expense worksheet
- Instructions for writing a sales and marketing proposal
- Instructions for writing a press release
- Press release samples
- Template of a proposal to a client
- Main client information sheet
- Client information sheet for clients to fill out
- Invoice template

Web links
-